LABOR RELATIONS AND PUBLIC POLICY SERIES

NO. 23

OPERATING DURING STRIKES:
Company Experience, NLRB Policies, and Governmental Regulations

by

CHARLES R. PERRY

ANDREW M. KRAMER   THOMAS J. SCHNEIDER

INDUSTRIAL RESEARCH UNIT
The Wharton School, Vance Hall/CS
University of Pennsylvania
Philadelphia, Pennsylvania 19104
U.S.A.

Third Printing, 1983
© 1982 by the Trustees of the University of Pennsylvania
MANUFACTURED IN THE UNITED STATES OF AMERICA
Library of Congress Catalog Number 82-80521
ISBN: 0-89546-036-x
ISSN: 0075-7470

Foreword

The dramatic handling of the flight controllers' strike by President Ronald Reagan and Secretary of Transportation Drew Lewis has called attention to a relatively new phenomenon in United States industrial relations—the determination of management to operate facilities when employees strike. The controllers' strike is a rather unique example of this trend, first because the employer in this situation is the federal government, and second because an objective of the governmental employer is the replacement of the striking controllers not only temporarily by managers and supervisors, but permanently by newly hired employees.

On the other hand, the events of the controllers' strike do resemble those discussed in this book in many ways. The federal government officials involved had decided that the Professional Air Traffic Controllers' Organization (PATCO) would surely strike unless its extraordinarily expensive demands were fully met. For tactical and economic reasons, the decision was made that the flight controllers' functions should be manned as well as possible, and a detailed strike plan to accomplish this was drawn up and published in the *Federal Register* (by the Carter Administration). Despite heavy costs, such as flight cancellations and delays, overtime compensation, postponement of research and managerial functions, and use of executive time—including that of the President and the Secretary of Transportation—the federal government seems to have accomplished its purpose of maintaining the ban against strikes by federal employees, of restraining the wage inflation of these employees and the potential of a general wage inflation, and of providing the means for the maintenance of the bulk of air traffic under safe conditions.

One could state the matter in a more succinct fashion. The federal government's handling of the PATCO strike is an investment in maintaining strike-free, sensible negotiations in federal service and in controlling labor costs. These are precisely the objectives of the companies whose experience is examined in this monograph. The federal government also discharged the strikers for violating the law, which proscribes strikes by federal employees. In the cases studied here, the strikers were engaging in their rights under the law when, in concert, they left their jobs. In nearly all the cases analyzed, the employer had neither the intention nor the desire to replace the strikers permanently; its objective was to offset union bargaining power and to provide products for its customers so that permanent loss of business could be minimized. Thus, nonbargaining-unit employees, not permanent new hires, are utilized for such operations.

Operating during strikes is not a new management tactic. Highly automated process industries, especially petroleum refineries and chemical plants, have done this for many years. As automation took hold in the electric, gas, and telephone utilities, operating during strikes also became commonplace there. What is new, however, is that such industries as paper manufacturing, restaurants, supermarkets, food manufacturing, shipyards, and many others, some of which are labor-intensive, have adopted this tactic. As the faculty staff of the Wharton Industrial Research Unit discerned this development, it determined that it was precisely the type of issue that deserved careful attention. Dr. Charles R. Perry, Associate Professor of Management and Industrial Relations at the Wharton School and Senior Faculty Research Associate in the Industrial Research Unit, took on the job. In 1980, he personally visited with, collected information on, and interviewed in depth the companies selected for the sample of those that had operated during strikes.

After Dr. Perry had written up his findings, it became very clear both to him and to the senior Industrial Research Unit staff that no complete analysis of the experience of operating during strikes would be useful without a thorough and sophisticated integration of the field findings with the myriad of laws and legal rulings that affect the decision to operate during strikes and of actions before, during, and incident thereto. We consider ourselves most fortunate, therefore, to have obtained the services of Andrew M. Kramer, Esq., and Dr. Thomas J. Schneider to address these aspects of the problem. Mr. Kramer is Managing Partner, Washington office, Seyfarth, Shaw, Fairweather & Geraldson. He received his J.D. degree from Northwestern University. He recently served as Cochairman of the American Bar Association Subcommittee on Civil Rights and Public Employment, and is also a very active counsel to management throughout the United States in all aspects of labor-legal matters. Mr. Kramer brought to the study not only legal expertise, but also practical knowledge and experience. He was ably assisted by the third coauthor, Dr. Schneider, an associate of the same law firm. Dr. Schneider is a graduate of Harvard University, received his Ph.D. in industrial sociology from Oxford University, and then his J.D. from the Harvard Law School.

This study, *Operating During Strikes*, is published as the twenty-third monograph in the Labor Relations and Public Policy Series, which the Wharton Industrial Research Unit inaugurated in 1968 as a means of examining issues and stimulating discussions in the complex and controversial areas of industrial relations and the regulation of labor-management issues. Twelve of these monographs, as well as a major portion of this one, deal with various aspects of the National Labor Relations Board's procedures and policies. The other ten explain significant and controversial issues such as welfare and strikes; opening the skilled construction trades to blacks; the Davis-Bacon Act; the labor-management situation in urban school systems; old age, handicapped, and Vietnam-era antidiscrimination legislation; the impact of the Occupational Safety and Health Act; the effects of the AT&T-EEO consent decree; and unions' rights to company information.

Professor Richard L. Rowan, Codirector of the Industrial Research Unit, read the manuscript and made several valuable suggestions. The manuscript was edited by Ms. Cheryl DellaPenna, the Industrial Research Unit's Chief Editor, and Mary T. Kiely prepared the index. The manuscript was typed in various stages by the Industrial Research Unit's secretarial staff and the word processing unit of Seyfarth, Shaw, Fairweather & Geraldson. Administrative matters were handled by the Unit's Office Manager, Mrs. Margaret E. Doyle.

Research for this book was financed by generous grants from the J. Howard Pew Freedom Trust in support of the Labor Relations and Public Policy Series, by grants from the Gulf, Rollin M. Gerstacker, and A. O. Smith foundations, by Mobil Oil Corporation, and by membership contributions from the ninety-five corporations that constitute the Industrial Research Unit's Research Advisory Group. Editing and publication of this book were financed by grants from the John M. Olin Foundation.

As in all works published by the Wharton Industrial Research Unit, the senior author is solely responsible for the research and for all opinions expressed, which should not be attributed to any organization with which he is affiliated, to the grantors, or to the University of Pennsylvania.

HERBERT R. NORTHRUP, *Director*
Industrial Research Unit
The Wharton School

Philadelphia
January 1982

TABLE OF CONTENTS

CHAPTER I

Introduction

Collective bargaining is, in the final analysis, a process of economic power accommodation. The foundation of this process in our system of free collective bargaining is the right of unions to strike and the right of managements to take a strike. Within this framework, public policy has been fairly tolerant of attempts by either party to lower its own strike costs and to raise those of its adversary. Thus, the law permits unions to accumulate strike funds and to accept financial aid from other unions, and permits managements to build strike inventories and, except in the case of airlines, to participate in limited mutual-aid arrangements. The law also tolerates efforts by both sides to manipulate the scope or timing of a test of economic power to their own advantage through devices such as coalition bargaining and selective strikes on the part of unions, and lockouts on the part of managements.

One option open to management in seeking to enhance its economic power in collective bargaining is the exercise of its right to do business during a strike by operating production facilities with nonstriking personnel. In theory, the right to operate during strikes gives management the ability to enhance greatly the economic power inherent in its basic right to take a strike. In practice, however, this right has not been widely exercised by management. There are two reasons for this. First, plant operation is often not technologically easy given the problems in recruiting enough nonstriking workers to man a struck facility. Second, plant operation is not institutionally popular given the strong antipathy of unions toward such action and the consequences that this will have in future labor-management relations.

The fact that plant operation generally is not feasible or popular does not mean that the right to operate is essentially meaningless in our system of collective bargaining. Plant operation has become an integral part of collective bargaining in at least two high-technology industries—telephone and oil—and is increasingly becoming an important element in collective bargaining in a third such industry—chemicals. The long-term general trend toward less labor-intensive operations and the growing ratio of salaried to hourly personnel suggest that the option of plant operation is technologically feasible in more industries and companies than has been perceived to be the case. Recent attempts at plant operation in the newspaper, paper, shipbuilding, and hotel industries support this view.

If the technological barriers to plant operation are indeed weakening, the major constraint to management will more than ever be institutional. Undoubtedly, the institutional problems associated with operation—short-run violence and long-run bitterness—continue to constitute a serious constraint on the exercise of the right to operate. Managements in a growing number of companies and industries, however, appear to be willing to confront these problems as a matter of philosophical principle, economic necessity, or both. The recent decisions of such firms as the *Washington Post* and the Newport News Shipbuilding and Dry Dock Company and of industries such as the paper industry on the west coast and the hotel industry in San Francisco to break with tradition by operating during a strike are indicative of this growing management resolve.

Overall, technological and institutional conditions in the early 1980s appear to favor expanded exercise of the right to operate as an asset to management power in collective bargaining. Thus, this seems an appropriate time to reassess the use and usefulness of operating during a strike, particularly because it has been almost twenty years since scholarly attention last focused on this little used and often maligned management option. In 1960, the Independent Study Group, commissioned by the Committee for Economic Development to do the research for its publication *The Public Interest in National Labor Policy*, apparently found conditions sufficiently favorable for the exercise of the right to operate to warrant the Group's explicit attention to that subject at the policy level.[1] Shortly thereafter, Professor John G. Hutchinson of Columbia University reported the results of his investigation of plant operation at the practical level in a book entitled *Management Under Strike Conditions*.[2] Since then, the literature of industrial relations has been silent on the subject of plant operation during strikes.

THE USE AND USEFULNESS OF PLANT OPERATION

This study examines the legal, institutional, logistical, and economic dimensions of the decision to operate a production facility during a

---

[1] COMMITTEE FOR ECONOMIC DEVELOPMENT, THE PUBLIC INTEREST IN NATIONAL LABOR POLICY (1961).

[2] JOHN G. HUTCHINSON, MANAGEMENT UNDER STRIKE CONDITIONS (1966).

strike from the viewpoint of management. Based primarily on the experience of companies that have operated facilities during strikes in recent years, the study focuses on five basic questions:

1. What legal constraints exist on the right of management to operate during a strike?

2. What considerations lead management to the decision to exercise its right to operate?

3. What are the major logistical problems confronting management in operating a struck facility?

4. What economic and tactical advantages accrue to management as a result of operation?

5. What are the long-run implications of plant operation for union bargaining power?

Unfortunately, no body of data on the extent and incidence of plant operation exists that would permit identification of all the firms that have attempted to operate during strikes. Thus, the selection of a set of firms for intensive study had to be made on the basis of public information and knowledge. Fifteen companies known to have operated a major production facility during a strike were selected for study based on two criteria: (1) frequency of operation, and (2) feasibility of operation. In choosing both criteria, diversity rather than similarity was the goal.

In each of the companies, interviews were conducted with management personnel through a combination of informal discussion and questioning based on a detailed interview guide. The interviews were augmented in most cases by a review of relevant formal policies and procedures and, when available, strike manuals, plans, logs, and other documents relating to specific operating experiences. All of those interviewed were assured that they and their companies would not be identified and that all statements made and documents provided would be treated as confidential. Given these assurances, most of those interviewed were quite forthcoming and, in some cases, positively enthusiastic in discussing their plant operation policies, practices, and problems.

Overall, the interviews produced an abundance of information on plant operating experience, including both generalizations based on multiple operating experiences and detailed accounts of specific operating experiences. The following chapters present the results of an attempt to analyze that information in terms of the basic patterns common to the diverse policies, practices, problems, and results of the firms studied, as well as those of several other firms, the operating experiences of which are a matter of public record. These patterns must be regarded more as a mode than a norm for firms attempting to operate during strikes.

CHAPTER II

The Law and Its Impact on
a Decision to Operate

Although business judgment will determine whether a company should operate during a strike, a number of legal considerations play an important role in the formulation and implementation of that decision. The intent of this chapter is to provide a general overview of the legal issues that require consideration either in deciding to operate or in operating a plant once that decision has been made. Many of the items mentioned in this chapter will be discussed in greater length in other chapters, when specific operating issues are examined.

The company facing a strike can view it from both an offensive and defensive posture. On the one hand, an employer can, in appropriate cases, use the law to maintain ingress and egress to its facility, limit the number of pickets, restrict where strikers can picket, and secure orders to bar acts of violence. On the other hand, an employer must be mindful of its legal obligations; the National Labor Relations Act (NLRA), Fair Labor Standards Act (FLSA), and various state and local laws regulate in detail the conduct of parties to a labor dispute.

Legal considerations arise in all phases of a strike. The impact of the law may be crucial in deciding whether a plant should be operated during a strike. Some legal issues may become significant only in the heat of operations. Finally, an employer faces legal constraints at the end of the strike and the consequent return to work of striking employees.

Anticipation of potential legal problems is essential in developing a sound plan of operations. Thus, all foreseeable legal questions should be considered in deciding whether to operate, and contingencies should be prepared in advance in order to avoid or to satisfy the legal demands if and when they arise.

THE BARGAINING DUTY

Section 8(d) of the NLRA[1] mandates in broad terms that parties bargain in good faith with respect to "wages, hours, and other terms

---

[1] 29 U.S.C. § 158(d) (1973).

5

and conditions of employment." The duty of the parties to bargain is a continuing one, and applies even when a union has gone on strike, or an employer has locked out its employees.[2] Thus, as a rule, employers and unions must, at the request of the other party, engage in good-faith collective bargaining regardless of the fact that an ongoing economic dispute is underway.

Union's Right to Information

Of course, if an absolute deadlock exists, the parties are not required to engage in fruitless or marathon bargaining. The circumstances of the particular bargaining process and the perceptions of the involved parties determine whether an impasse exists.[3] A long strike or successful operation during a strike may be viewed as changing the circumstances of the parties' relationship, and, thus in a sense, breaking any impasse that may exist.[4]

Topics that relate to wages, hours, and other terms and conditions of employment constitute mandatory subjects of bargaining. When raised by either party, mandatory bargaining subjects must be negotiated in good faith.[5] Furthermore, both parties can lawfully insist on such topics to the point of a bargaining impasse.[6] Once an impasse has been reached, an employer is free to implement unilaterally its final offer.[7]

An employer is under no obligation to bargain over a decision to train or to use strike replacements.[8] Similarly, an employer is not compelled to bargain over the use of economic weapons that it might choose to invoke during a labor dispute.[9]

Upon a union's request, however, an employer may have a duty to disclose certain information arising out of the duty to bargain. Specifically, a union may request information about personnel being

---

[2] *See* NLRB v. Rutter-Rex Mfg. Co., 245 F.2d 594, 596 (5th Cir. 1957).

[3] *See* Cheney Calif. Lumber Co. v. NLRB, 319 F.2d 375, 380 (9th Cir. 1963) (the standard for an impasse is "whether [an involved party had reasonable cause to believe and did sincerely believe that] an impasse had been reached."); Alsey Refractories Co., 215 N.L.R.B. 785 (1974) where the National Labor Relations Board applied the more objective test of whether the respondent was "warranted in assuming that further bargaining would have been futile."

[4] *See* NLRB v. Reed & Prince Mfg. Co., 118 F.2d 874 (1st Cir. 1941); NLRB v. United States Cold Storage Corp., 203 F. 2d 924 (5th Cir. 1953), *cert. denied,* 346 U.S. 818 (1953).

[5] *See* NLRB v. Wooster Div. of Borg-Warner Corp., 356 U.S. 342 (1958).

[6] *Id.*

[7] *See* NLRB v. Crompton Highland Mills, Inc., 337 U.S. 217, 224-225 (1949); Bi-Rite Foods, Inc., 147 N.L.R.B. 59, 64-65 (1964).

[8] *See generally* Times Pub. Co., 72 N.L.R.B. 676 (1947); Hawaii Meat Co. v. NLRB, 321 F.2d 397 (9th Cir. 1963).

[9] *See* R. GORMAN, LABOR LAW: UNIONIZATION AND COLLECTIVE BARGAINING 431-34 (1976).

trained by the employer to fill specific jobs in the event of a strike. In recent years, the National Labor Relations Board (NLRB) has faced the issue of an employer's duty to disclose information about such training programs.

Employers are generally obliged to furnish unions, upon request, with any information the employer has that is relevant to the union's role as a bargaining agent.[10] The obligation continues during a strike. Failure by an employer to observe this obligation constitutes an unfair labor practice under section 8(a)(5) of the NLRA.[11]

Both the NLRB and the federal courts consider wage and related information to be presumptively relevant, and the employer bears the burden of showing a lack of relevance.[12] Information sought for nonbargaining-unit personnel does not enjoy the same presumption of relevance, and the union bears the burden of showing that it is relevant to negotiable issues.[13]

Training Information

Against this general standard, the NLRB and federal courts have decided on whether an employer is obligated to provide a union with the names of employees who are being trained to perform certain jobs in the event of a strike and with information relating to such a training program. For example, in *San Diego Newspaper Guild Local No. 95 v. NLRB*,[14] the union sought the names of nonbargaining-unit employees who the employer was training to operate its newspaper in the event of a strike. Because the individuals being trained were outside the bargaining unit, the burden was on the union to establish relevancy. Satisfaction of this burden required showing that the training program was in violation of the collective bargaining agreement or that the information was necessary for negotiations. The Board and the Ninth Circuit Court of Appeals both found that the union's claim of relevance could not be supported, and that the refusal to furnish the information did not violate the Act.

In *A. S. Abell Co.*,[15] a similar issue was presented in a somewhat different context. There, an employer offered cross-training to employees in one bargaining unit in preparation for a potential strike by em-

---

[10] *See generally* J.T. O'REILLY, UNIONS' RIGHTS TO COMPANY INFORMATION (1980).

[11] 29 U.S.C. § 158(a)(5) (1973).

[12] *See generally* NLRB v. Central Mach. and Tool Co., Inc., 429 F.2d 1127 (10th Cir. 1970), *cert. denied,* 401 U.S. 909 (1971).

[13] *See* NLRB v. Rockwell-Standard Corp., 410 F.2d 953, 957 (6th Cir. 1960).

[14] 548 F.2d 863 (9th Cir. 1977), *enforcing* 220 N.L.R.B. 1226 (1975).

[15] 230 N.L.R.B. 1112 (1977).

ployees in another unit. The union representing employees in the bargaining unit being offered the training sought information relating to the program and the names of those being trained. When the employer refused to provide the information, an unfair labor practice charge was filed.

Finding that the information sought was relevant, the Board ordered the employer to provide the information. The Board's decision was premised on the fact that the information sought was needed to assist the union in enforcing its collecting bargaining agreement and in preparing itself for future negotiations. On appeal, this ruling was reversed.[16]

In the above case, the United States Court of Appeals for the Fourth Circuit first held that, even assuming that the information was relevant, the company had rebutted the presumption by showing that the union had previously misused similar information. This finding was predicated on the fact that, at an earlier point in time, when the union had been given names of employees who had been cross-trained, the union had harassed the employees and had not used the data for either bargaining or contract administration purposes. Although this ground was sufficient to dispose of the case, the court went on to hold that the union had not demonstrated any basis for its request other than a bald assertion that the training might conflict with its collective bargaining agreement. To the court, such an assertion was insufficient; the union needed to demonstrate why the information was necessary to its role as bargaining agent.

These decisions reflect some of the tensions posed by unions' requests for information when employers plan to operate during a strike. The *Abell* and *San Diego* cases illustrate that, regarding training information, the NLRB at least will view requests differently when training is for employees outside the unit than when bargaining-unit employees are being trained.

RIGHTS OF STRIKERS UNDER THE NLRA

The National Labor Relations Act essentially characterizes three different types of strikes: economic strikes, unfair labor practice strikes, and illegal or unprotected strikes. Understanding the distinctions among these different types of strikes, and the rights of employees engaging in one type of strike or another, is important for an employer attempting to operate during a strike.

---

[16] 624 F.2d 506 (4th Cir. 1980).

Lawful Strikes

As a preliminary matter, in order to strike lawfully, a union must first comply with the statutory notice requirements set forth in section 8(d) of the NLRA.[17] Section 8(d) provides for statutory notice requirements prior to the modification or termination of a labor contract. This section of the Act essentially specifies that, when a collective bargaining agreement is in effect, the party seeking to modify or terminate the agreement is required to follow certain steps. These include giving written notice sixty days in advance of an intent to modify or terminate and notifying the federal and state mediation and conciliation services within thirty days after giving the initial notice.

If a union should strike before both the sixty-day and thirty-day statutory notice requirements are met, a distinct scheme of remedies becomes available. A failure to give statutory section 8(d) notice before commencing a strike is a refusal to bargain in good faith, and thus, a section 8(b)(3) violation.[18] Employees who strike in violation of section 8(d) engage in unprotected activity under section 7, and, therefore, may be permanently discharged;[19] also, an unfair labor practice charge may be filed accompanied with a request that the Board seek injunctive relief against the strike.

Economic Strikes

Economic strikes are the type normally faced by an employer. These strikes are protected under section 7 of the NLRA.[20] Economic strikers cannot be discharged solely because they are on strike, but they may be replaced. An employer may hire permanent replacements for striking employees in order to "protect and continue his business."[21] Although an unfair labor practice striker may, upon request, return to the job,[22] an economic striker may be replaced. The economic striker, however, enjoys preferential rights of rehire.[23]

An employer may not pay either temporary or permanent strike replacements more than it was paying the employees who went out on strike, or if negotiations reached a bona fide impasse, more than the

---

[17] 29 U.S.C. § 158(d) (1973).

[18] *See* NLRB v. Local 742, Elec. Workers, 519 F.2d 815 (6th Cir. 1975), *enforcing* 213 N.L.R.B. 824 (1974).

[19] *See* United Furniture Workers v. NLRB, 336 F.2d 738 (D.C. Cir.), *cert. denied*, 379 U.S. 838 (1964).

[20] 29 U.S.C. § 157 (1973).

[21] NLRB v. Mackay Radio & Tel. Co., 304 U.S. 333, 345 (1938).

[22] *See* Mastro Plastics Corp. v. NLRB, 350 U.S. 270 (1956).

[23] *See* Laidlaw Corp. v. NLRB, 414 F.2d 99 (7th Cir. 1969), *cert. denied*, 397 U.S. 920 (1970).

last offer made by the employer to the union.[24] This rule continues after the strike.

Employees who are members of nonstriking bargaining units and who work during a labor dispute must receive the terms and conditions of employment set forth in the collective bargaining agreements that currently apply to them. Members of the involved bargaining unit who work during the dispute should continue to receive the same terms and conditions that were provided for in the expired agreement.

Unfair Labor Practice Strikes

When a strike is caused or prolonged by an employer's unfair labor practice, striking employees have, as noted above, the right to request and secure reinstatement at the end of the strike. Thus, an employer cannot permanently replace an unfair labor practice striker.

Illegal or Unprotected Strikes

Unlike employees who engage in either economic or unfair labor practice strikes, those who engage in illegal or unprotected strike activity do not enjoy the protection of section 7 of the NLRA. If an employee strikes in violation of a contractual no-strike clause or in violation of the notice requirements of section 8(d), an employer is generally free to discharge that employee.[25]

Sympathy Actions

For purposes of the Act, the status of strikers takes on particular meaning when an employer is operating during a strike and when certain groups of employees, individually or collectively, honor picket lines established by the striking union. For many years the NLRB has held that employees have a right under section 7 of the Act to honor a picket line.[26] Recent court decisions have affirmed the notion that nonstriking employees "who refuse as a matter of principle to cross a picket line . . . have plighted [their] troth with the strikers,"[27] and thereby retain the rights accorded the striking employees.

The right to engage in a sympathy strike may, however, be waived in

---

[24] *See* NLRB v. Crompton-Highland Mills, 337 U.S. 217 (1949); Harold Hinson d/b/a/ Henhouse Market No. 3, 175 N.L.R.B. 596 (1969), *aff'd,* 428 F.2d 133 (8th Cir. 1970).

[25] *See* NLRB v. Sands Mfg. Co., 306 U.S. 332 (1939); United Furniture Workers v. NLRB, 336 F.2d 738 (D.C. Cir.), *cert. denied,* 379 U.S. 838 (1964).

[26] *See, e.g.,* Cyril de Cordova & Bros., 91 N.L.R.B. 1121 (1950); Redwig Carriers, Inc., 137 N.L.R.B. 1545, *enforced,* 325 F.2d 1011 (D.C. Cir. 1963), *cert. denied,* 377 U.S. 905 (1964).

[27] NLRB v. Southern Greyhound Lines, 426 F.2d 1299, 1301 (5th Cir. 1970).

a collective bargaining agreement.[28] Whether the right has been waived may become a matter for interpretation by either an arbitrator, the NLRB, or a federal court.[29] For purposes of the NLRA, the NLRB and the courts require a showing of a clear and unmistakable waiver of the right to engage in a sympathy strike.[30]

An employer planning to operate during a strike, therefore, must be sensitive to the rights afforded nonbargaining-unit employees. Consideration must be given to the possibility that certain groups of employees who are represented by a nonstriking union might also refuse to work. Later in this chapter we discuss how a no-strike pledge may be enforced to secure a return of such employees.

RIGHT TO UTILIZE MANAGERIAL AND SUPERVISORY PERSONNEL

For purposes of this discussion, managerial and supervisory employees must be distinguished from employees protected by section 7. Generally, an employer may require management and supervisory personnel to continue working during a labor dispute without regard to their membership or nonmembership in a union. Moreover, an employer is not restricted regarding the kind of work it may assign these individuals to perform. Thus, an employer does not commit an unfair labor practice by disciplining or discharging managerial or supervisory personnel who refuse to perform work for the employer during a labor dispute, regardless of whether the work is supervisory or nonsupervisory in nature.[31]

Because of the legal significance of utilizing managerial and supervisory employees during a labor dispute, a company must determine which members of its work force actually are managerial employees or supervisors under the National Labor Relations Act.

Managerial Status and Confidential Employees

Members of management have been held not to be employees within the meaning of the NLRA.[32] Therefore, they do not have the rights afforded employees under that Act, such as honoring a picket line.

---

[28] *See* NLRB v. Rockaway News Supply Co., 345 U.S. 71 (1953).

[29] *See generally* R. GORMAN, *supra,* note 9, at 324-25.

[30] *See* Gary-Hobart Water Corp., 210 N.L.R.B. 742, 744 (1974), *enforced,* 511 F.2d 284 (7th Cir.), *cert. denied,* 423 U.S. 925 (1975); Local 18, Operating Engineers (Davis McKee, Inc.), 238 N.L.R.B. No. 58 (1978); Pacemaker Yacht Company, 253 N.L.R.B. No. 95 (1980), *enforcement denied,* 108 L.R.R.M. 2817 (3d Cir. 1981).

[31] *See* Texas Co. v. NLRB, 198 F.2d 540 (9th Cir. 1952).

[32] *See* NLRB v. Bell Aerospace Co., 416 U.S. 267 (1974), *on remand,* 219 N.L.R.B. 384 (1975).

Usually, whether a particular individual is "management" by virtue of his title, status, or duties is without question. In many instances, however, the determination is far more difficult, and the problem is compounded by the fact that the statute gives no guidance as to when an individual will be considered to be "managerial." Thus, the NLRB and the courts have fashioned a definition of managerial status. The NLRB articulated the following definition of management-level employees as:

> Those who formulate and effectuate management policies by expressing and making operative the decisions of their employer, and those who have discretion in the performance of their jobs independent of their employer's established policy . . . managerial status is not conferred upon rank-and-file workers, or upon those who perform routinely, but rather it is reserved for those in executive-type positions, those who are closely aligned with management as true representatives of management.[33]

The application of this definition involves a careful assessment of an individual's actual job responsibilities, authority, and relationship to other members of management. Because of the difficulties in applying this definition and the potentially substantial monetary liability of an employer that, during a labor dispute, discharges an employee improperly classified as managerial, counsel should be consulted before taking any such action.

A second area of difficulty in determining managerial status relates to the exclusion of confidential employees from protection under the Act.[34] The traditional standards for determining whether an employee has a confidential relationship with the employer is whether the employee assists and acts in a confidential capacity to persons responsible for labor policy[35] or has access to confidential information that may relate to collective bargaining negotiations.[36] This standard has now been affirmed by the Supreme Court in *Hendricks County Rural Electric Membership Corp. v. NLRB.*[37] In *Hendricks*, the Court declined to broaden the definition of confidentiality beyond the traditional labor nexus standard, thus refusing to include employees with access to any confidential matter, including information concerning competitors, regulatory agencies, and the public.

---

[33] 219 N.L.R.B. at 385 (citation omitted).
[34] *See* Ford Motor Co., 66 N.L.R.B. 1317 (1946); The B.F. Goodrich Co., 115 N.L.R.B. 722 (1956).
[35] The B.F. Goodrich Co., 115 N.L.R.B. 722, 724 (1956).
[36] Pullman Standard Division, 214 N.L.R.B. 762 (1974).
[37] 50 U.S.L.W. 4037 (December 1, 1981).

Supervisory Status

The NLRA expressly excludes supervisors from the definition of "employee." Supervisors, therefore, do not have the same statutory rights as employees. Section 2(11) of the Act defines a "supervisor" as:

> Any individual having authority, in the interest of the employer, to hire, transfer, suspend, layoff, recall, promote, discharge, assign, reward, or discipline other employees, or responsibly direct them, or to adjust their grievances, or effectively to recommend such action, if in connection with the foregoing the exercise of such authority is not of a merely routine or clerical nature, but requires the use of independent judgment.[38]

In determining which individuals are supervisors, the following general principles should be considered.

1. As a practical matter, the single most important criterion in the definition is the authority to hire and fire, or to make effective recommendations as to hiring and firing. Supervisory status, however, often is shown by evidence of effective authority in the other areas included within the definition. Moreover, the individual in question need not have authority in all of the areas for supervisory status to be established.[39]

2. In determining supervisory status, the appearances of authority, such as job title, will not be controlling; rather, an analysis must be made as to whether the person actually exercises independent judgment and discretion in hiring, firing, and directing the work of other employees.[40]

3. The NLRB usually will find that one who possesses the type of authority described in the statute is a supervisor, even though such authority is exercised infrequently. Thus, an individual who spends most of his time engaged in nonsupervisory work, but who also exercises or has the authority to exercise legitimate supervisory functions, may still be considered a supervisor.[41]

4. The performance of duties of a supervisory nature on a sporadic, irregular, or infrequent basis does not, however, transform an employee into a supervisor.[42] An employee does not acquire supervisory status merely by taking over supervisory duties

---

[38] 29 U.S.C. § 152 (11).

[39] *See* Arizona Public Service Co. v. NLRB, 453 F.2d 228 (9th Cir. 1971).

[40] International Union of Elec. Workers v. NLRB, 426 F.2d 1243 (D.C. Cir.), *cert. denied,* 400 U.S. 950 (1970).

[41] *See* American Cable & Radio Corp., 121 N.L.R.B. 258 (1958).

[42] *See* NLRB v. Lindsay Newspapers, Inc., 315 F.2d 709 (5th Cir. 1963).

when a supervisor is occasionally absent.[43] On the other hand, an individual who substitutes for a supervisor on a regular basis (e.g., one day a week) and exercises real supervisory authority on such occasions usually will be considered a supervisor.[44] Although the determination of supervisory status often is less difficult and complex than that of managerial status, many factors of varying relevance must be considered in any specific situation.

COMMUNICATIONS TO BARGAINING-UNIT EMPLOYEES DURING A LABOR DISPUTE

During the course of a strike, an employer may want to communicate with its employees. The NLRA guarantees employers the right of free speech, including the right to communicate directly with employees about collective bargaining and strike issues during a strike. But this right is not absolute. The law prohibits employer communications that are intended to undermine or bypass the union as the employees' exclusive collective bargaining representative.[45] This prohibition extends to threats or promises that are intended to erode support for the union among employees.[46]

Although these general rules are well established, precise definition of what is and what is not a lawful communication is extremely difficult. Therefore, each communication, and the factual circumstances surrounding it, must be analyzed by counsel. In addition, before a communication is released, all supervisors and management personnel should be advised of its content in order to enable them to respond to employee or public reaction to the communication.

The following examples provide guidance as to the types of communications that have been found lawful and unlawful.

Communications Regarding Collective Bargaining Issues

The question presented most often regarding collective bargaining issues is whether a communication is an attempt by the employer to

---

[43] *See* Murphy Bonded Warehouse, Inc., 180 N.L.R.B. 463 (1969).

[44] *See, e.g.,* White Chapel Memorial Ass'n, 167 N.L.R.B. 926 (1967), *aff'd,* 414 F.2d 236 (6th Cir. 1969).

[45] NLRB v. General Electric Co., 418 F.2d 736 (2d Cir. 1969), *cert. denied,* 397 U.S. 965 (1970).

[46] *See* 29 U.S.C. § 158(c) (1973); Youngstown Sheet and Tube Co., 238 N.L.R.B. 1082 (1978); Swarco, Inc. v. NLRB, 303 F.2d 668 (6th Cir. 1962), *cert. denied,* 373 U.S. 931 (1963).

undermine the union by bargaining directly with the employees. If it is, the communication is not permitted.

Permissible Communications. Employers have been found to have acted lawfully when they:

1. accurately informed employees of the status of negotiations and stated the employer's position;[47]

2. clarified confusion as to certain contract proposals, answered employee questions involving interpretations or understanding of the proposed contract, and informed employees of the employer's concern over the possibility of a work stoppage;[48] and

3. asked employees to vote to accept the employer's final offer when it was presented for ratification.[49]

Impermissible Communications. Employers have been found to have acted unlawfully when they:

1. offered directly to employees, during a representation of negotiations, a contract of greater economic value than any previously offered to the union;[50]

2. appealed directly to employees during an impasse in collective bargaining negotiations for a "partnership solution" to the problem;[51] and

3. misrepresented the union's bargaining position to the employees by implying that the union's contract proposals were in some respect adverse to their interests, and then suggested that the employees decide among themselves whether they should sign the contract.[52]

Communications Regarding Strike Issues

The question presented most often regarding strike issues is whether a communication is an attempt by the employer to threaten or induce employees to leave the union or to abandon their bargaining agent during the course of a strike. In this regard, threats and promises by overzealous supervisors to induce individual strikers to return to work are common unfair labor practices.

---

[47] *See* Wantagh Auto Sales, Inc., 177 N.L.R.B. 150 (1969).
[48] *See* Stokely-Van Camp, Inc., 186 N.L.R.B. 440 (1970).
[49] *See* NLRB v. Movie Star, Inc., 361 F.2d 346 (5th Cir. 1966).
[50] *See* AMF Inc.-Union Mach. Div., 219 N.L.R.B. 903 (1975).
[51] *See* NLRB v. Goodyear Aerospace Corp., 497 F.2d 747 (6th Cir. 1974).
[52] *See* Colony Furniture Co., 144 N.L.R.B. 1582 (1963).

Permissible Communications.   Employers have been found to have acted lawfully when they:

1. advised striking employees that their jobs were available to them and that their best interest was served by abandoning the strike;[53]

2. informed striking employees that permanent replacements would be hired but that strikers could return to work before their jobs were filled;[54] and

3. sent letters to strikers in which the company's bargaining position was explained and, without threats or coercion, requested strikers to return to work.[55]

Impermissible Communications.   Employers have been found to have acted unlawfully when they:

1. offered a raise to employees to discourage them from joining a strike;[56]

2. sent a letter to striking employees that threatened a loss of seniority benefits if they continued to strike;[57] and

3. promised increased benefits to strikers if they abandoned the strike and told the strikers that the employer would not settle with the union.[58]

TREATMENT OF CONTRACTUAL AND LEGALLY REQUIRED BENEFITS

The NLRB and the courts have consistently adhered to the principle that an employer need not compensate strikers for work not performed. An employer, therefore, may lawfully withhold from strikers wages and benefits in the nature of wages as long as those wages or benefits were not accrued prior to the initiation of a strike. The principles applicable to the status of wages and benefits during a strike are also generally applicable in the case of a lawful lockout.[59]

---

[53] *See* American Welding & Industrial Sales, Inc., 214 N.L.R.B. 1086 (1974).

[54] *See* Valley Oil Co., 210 N.L.R.B. 370 (1974).

[55] *See* Kansas Milling Co. v. NLRB, 185 F.2d 413 (10th Cir. 1950).

[56] *See* Harris-Teeter Supermarkets, Inc., 242 N.L.R.B. 132 (1979), *enforced,* 106 L.R.R.M. 3076 (D.C. Cir. 1981).

[57] *See* Lockwoven Co., 245 N.L.R.B. No. 178 (1979), *enforced,* 622 F.2d 296 (8th Cir. 1980).

[58] *See* SKRL Die Casting, Inc., 245 N.L.R.B. No. 134 (1979).

[59] *See* Sargent-Welch Scientific Co., 208 N.L.R.B. 811 (1974).

Wages

Employees who engage in a strike generally are entitled under state law to be paid all wages that they earned prior to the strike. Employees who honor a picket line of another union are considered to be sympathy strikers, and, as such, would be entitled to their accrued wages on the same basis as primary strikers.

Health, Welfare, and Pension-Fund Payments

Absent a contractual agreement to the contrary, an employer may lawfully discontinue payments on behalf of a striking employee to health, welfare, and pension funds.[60] Certain state laws require that an employer notify its striking employees of an intent to discontinue coverage for medical, surgical, or hospital benefits. For example, section 2806 of the California Labor Code provides that:

> No employer, whether private or public, shall discontinue coverage for medical, surgical, or hospital benefits for employees unless the employer has notified and advised all covered employees in writing of any discontinuation of coverage, inclusive of nonrenewal and cancellation, but not inclusive of employment termination or cases in which substitute coverage has been provided, at least 15 days in advance of such discontinuation.
>
> If coverage is provided by a third party, failure of the employer to give the necessary notice shall not require the third party to continue the coverage beyond the date it would otherwise terminate.[61]

This statute is not applicable to plans covered by the Employment Retirement Income Security Act (ERISA). Under ERISA, an employer appears to have no obligation with respect to the continuation of payments to plans during a labor dispute.

Life and Disability Insurance

Absent a contractual agreement to the contrary, an employer may lawfully discontinue payment of life or disability insurance premiums for striking employees.[62] Again, certain states require that any group life or disability insurance policy that is paid in whole or in part by an employer pursuant to a collective bargaining agreement must give a striking employee the right to keep the coverage and pay the contribution that would otherwise be made by the employer.[63]

---

[60] *See* General Electric Co., 80 N.L.R.B. 510 (1948); Trading Port, Inc., 219 N.L.R.B. 298, 299 n.3 (1975).

[61] Cal. Labor Code § 2806 (West).

[62] *See* Simplex Wire & Cable Company, 245 N.L.R.B. No. 85 (1979).

[63] *See, e.g.,* Cal. Ins. Code § 10116 (1972).

Sickness and Accident Benefits

Whether a striking employee is entitled to receive sickness and accident benefits, including sick leave and disability payments, depends on whether the benefits are judged to be accrued benefits or to be a form of wages. Accrued benefits must be paid during a strike;[64] wage equivalent benefits may be withheld.[65] The language of the collective bargaining agreement may influence how the benefits are classified.

Absent clear contractual language to the contrary, employees who are receiving accrued sickness and accident benefits are entitled to continue to receive these benefits during a labor dispute as long as the employees are disabled.[66] The ruling on public support, or lack of support, for a strike from disabled employees was expanded to hold that, even when disabled employees evidence support for a strike, a company's obligation to continue paying the benefits is not lessened.[67] These decisions pose practical problems for a company facing a strike. Increased numbers of employees may claim injuries in order to obtain sickness and accident benefits in anticipation of a strike.

Seniority

When discussing seniority-type benefits that may lawfully be denied employees engaged in a labor dispute, the NLRB and the courts distinguish between net credited service and seniority. Net credited service is the amount of time actually worked by the employee. Seniority is usually the amount of time that has elapsed from the employee's hire date. Net credited service often is used to determine the length of vacations, entitlement to pensions, sick benefits, and termination pay. Seniority usually relates to choice of vacation time, promotion eligibility, choice of hours, and order of layoff and recall.[68] Generally, an employer may lawfully stop the accrual of net credited service for employees engaged in a labor dispute during the term of that dispute. An employer cannot lawfully deny such employees the accrual of seniority for the period of the dispute if nonparticipating employees are permitted to accrue seniority for the same period.

---

[64] *See* NLRB v. Great Dane Trailers, Inc., 388 U.S. 26 (1967); E.L. Wiegand Div., Emerson Electric Co. v. NLRB, 650 F.2d 463 (3d Cir. 1981); Indiana & Michigan Electric Co., 236 N.L.R.B. 986 (1978), *enf'd without opinion,* 610 F.2d 812 (4th Cir. 1979).

[65] *See* Southwestern Electric Power Co., 216 N.L.R.B. 522 (1975).

[66] E.L. Wiegand Division, Emerson Electric Co., 246 N.L.R.B. No. 162 (1979), *enf'd,* 650 F.2d 463 (3d Cir. 1981).

[67] *See* E.L. Wiegand Div., Emerson Electric Co. v. NLRB, 650 F.2d 463 (3d Cir. 1981).

[68] *See* General Electric Co., 80 N.L.R.B. 510 (1948).

Vacations

If under the contract entitlement to vacation time is based on net credited service, the time during a labor dispute when an involved employee is off work need not be considered when computing vacation benefits.[69] If under the contract entitlement to vacation is based only on service or seniority, however, an employer may be required to count the employee's time off when computing entitlement to vacation benefits.[70]

An employer's right to reschedule vacations or deny vacations during a labor dispute depends upon the interpretation of the relevant agreement, past practice, and business justification.[71]

Holidays

Under federal law, holiday pay is viewed as wages; therefore, strikers would not be entitled to such pay.

Whether sympathy strikers and laid-off employees who are covered by other collective bargaining agreements have the right to receive holiday pay depends upon the interpretation of the applicable agreements and the past practice of the parties. For example, some agreements require that an employee work certain shifts in order to receive holiday pay. Arbitrators generally have held that, under these types of agreements, employees are not entitled to holiday pay if they have failed to work the required shifts because of their direct or indirect participation in a labor dispute.[72]

Unemployment Compensation Benefits

National labor policy has long been predicated on avoiding governmental intrusion into the collective bargaining process.[73] Negotiation of an agreement should be based on the respective abilities of the parties to withstand the economic pressures generated by a dispute without government aid or intervention. Nonetheless, in recent years a

---

[69] *See* Ohio Power Co., 63 Lab. Arb. 1235 (1974) (Chockley, Arb.); Pabst Brewing Co., 76-2 Lab. Arb. Awards (CCH) ¶ 8291 (1976) (Richman, Arb.).

[70] *See* Mobil Oil Co., 68-2 Lab. Arb. Awards (CCH) ¶ 8480 (1968) (Davis, Arb.); Butler Mfr. Co., 67-2 Lab. Arb. Awards (CCH) ¶ 8510 (1967) (Vickery, Arb.). This case involved a plant that operated during a strike while scheduling work as normal. Vacations were tied to service time, which, in turn, was calculated from the days of scheduled work.

[71] *See, e.g.,* Combustion Engineering Inc., 61 Lab. Arb. 1061 (1973) (Altrock, Arb.).

[72] *See, e.g.,* Gregory Galvanizing & Metal Processing, Inc., 46 Lab. Arb. 102 (1966) (Kates, Arb.).

[73] *See generally* NLRB v. Ins. Agents Int'l Union, 361 U.S. 477, 490 (1960); H.K. Porter Co. v. NLRB, 397 U.S. 99, 104 (1970); NLRB v. American Nat'l Ins., 343 U.S. 395, 408-09 (1952).

number of governmental programs have become available to strikers.[74] One such form of benefit is unemployment compensation. Strikers are generally denied unemployment compensation benefits, but special rules come into play when an employer decides to operate during a strike. Because of the potential impact of such benefits, companies should carefully examine the specific laws and judicial decisions of the state or states in which they have operations. In general, state laws in this area can be grouped into three categories.

Two states, New York and Rhode Island, specifically permit strikers to receive unemployment compensation. The United States Supreme Court in *New York Telephone Co. v. New York State Department of Labor*[75] recently upheld the constitutionality of the New York laws, finding that state regulation in this area is not preempted by federal labor law. Under the current New York and Rhode Island laws, strikers must wait eight and seven weeks, respectively, after the start of a strike to begin collecting unemployment benefits. Strikers under the separate federal railroad plan may receive benefits while on strike within one week after they leave their jobs.

About one-half of the states make an individual who is out of work because of a labor dispute ineligible for unemployment compensation.[76] These states focus on the individual employee: if an employee is voluntarily not working because he is participating in a labor dispute, he does not get unemployment compensation. The operational level of the employer's business is inconsequential in determining whether or not employees get unemployment compensation.[77] Questions may arise under this approach regarding what actually constitutes a "labor dispute."

---

[74] *See generally* ITT Lamp Div. v. Minter, 435 F.2d 989 (1st Cir. 1970), *cert. denied,* 402 U.S. 933 (1971) (upholding state's payment of welfare to strikers). *See also* Super Tire Eng'r Co. v. McCorkle, 550 F.2d 903 (3d Cir.), *cert. denied,* 434 U.S. 827 (1977); A. THIEBLOT & R. COWIN, WELFARE AND STRIKES: THE USE OF PUBLIC FUNDS TO SUPPORT STRIKERS (1972).

[75] 440 U.S. 519 (1979).

[76] *See* Ala. Code Tit. 25, § 4-78 (Supp. 1980); Alaska Stat. § 23.20.380(9) (1972); Ariz. Rev. Stat. § 23-777 (1971); Ark. Stat. Ann. § 81-1105 (1976); Cal. Unemp. Ins. Code § 1962 (Deering) (1971); Colo. Rev. Stat. § 8-73-109 (1973 & Supp. 1978); Conn. Gen. Stat. Ann. § 31-236(3) (West Supp. 1980); D.C. Code Ann. § 46-310(f) (1967 & Supp. VII 1980); Fla. Stat. Ann. § 443.06(4) (West 1966 & Supp. 1980); Idaho Code § 72-1366(h) (Supp. 1980); Ind. Code § 22-4-15-3 (Supp. 1980); Ky. Rev. Stat. Ann. § 341,360(1) (Baldwin 1979); La. Rev. Stat. Ann. § 23.1601(4) (West 1964); Mich. Stat. Ann. § 17.531(8) (1975); Minn. Stat. Ann. § 268.09(3) (West Supp. 1980); Nev. Rev. Stat. § 612.395 (1973); N.H. Stat. Ann. § 51-1-7(D) (1979); N.C. Gen. Stat. § 96-14(5) (1975); Ohio Rev. Code Ann. § 4141.29(d) (Page 1980); Or. Rev. Stat. § 657.200 (1979); S.C. Code § 41-35-120(4) (1977); Tenn. Code Ann. § 50-1324(D); Tex. Rev. Civ. Stat. Ann. art. 5211b-3(d) (Supp. 1979); Va. Code § 60-1-52(b) (Supp. 1980); Wis. Stat. Ann. § 108.04(10) (West 1974).

[77] *See generally* Leach v. Republic Steel Corp., 176 Ohio St. 221, 27 Ohio Op.2d 122, 199 N.E.2d 3 (1964).

The remaining states generally adopt a "stoppage of work" approach.[78] These laws, modeled on the laws governing unemployment compensation for strikers in Great Britain, primarily focus on whether a given labor dispute has caused a work stoppage at the employer's place of business rather than on the work stoppage by the individual employee. In essence, this approach involves a two-pronged analysis beginning with a determination of whether a labor dispute exists and then a determination of whether the given labor dispute has resulted in a work stoppage at the employer's place of business. If a labor dispute results in a work stoppage, employees unemployed because of the dispute cannot receive unemployment benefits. If the dispute does not result in a work stoppage, as so defined under the relevant statutes and judicial interpretations, employees unemployed as a result of the dispute may receive unemployment benefits.[79] In either case, work must be available for the striking employees to perform in order to disqualify those employees from unemployment benefits.

Thus, the critical determination under such statutory provisions is what constitutes a work stoppage. Obviously, if an employer, through replacements or managerial or supervisory personnel, is able to run his plant at normal capacity, no work stoppage will be found and striking employees may receive unemployment benefits. At less than normal capacity, the outcome will vary by state.

Courts in different states have arrived at different conclusions regarding the level of operation necessary before a striking employee is eligible for unemployment compensation. Generally, the critical question is how much the firm's production of goods or services has decreased because of the strike. As a rule of thumb, if total output has decreased by more than about 25 percent because of the labor dispute, courts are likely to hold striking employees ineligible for unemployment compensation.[80] On the other hand, if total production decreased by less than 25 percent, courts may find no "stoppage of work," and

---

[78] *See* Del. Code Tit. 19, § 3315(4) (1979); Ga. Code Ann. § 54-610(d) (Supp. 1980); Haw. Rev. Stat. § 383-30(4) (1976); Ill. Rev. Stat. Ann. ch. 48, § 434 (Supp. 1980-81); Iowa Code Ann. § 96.5 (West Supp. 1980-81); Kan. Tit. 26, § 1193(4) (1974 & Supp. 1980-81); Md. Ann. Code Art. 95 A, § 6(e) (1979); Mass. Ann. Laws ch. 151 A, § 25(b) (Michie/Law Co-op 1976); Miss. Code Ann. § 71-5-513(5) (1973); Mo. Ann. Stat. § 288.040(5) (Vernon Supp. 1980); Mont. Rev. Codes Ann. § 39-51-2305 (1979); Neb. Rev. Stat. § 48-628 (Supp. 1977); N.H. Rev. Stat. Ann. § 282:4 (1966 & Supp. 1979); N.J. Stat. Ann. § 43:21-5 (West Supp. 1980-81); N.D. Cent. Code § 52-0602(4) (Supp. 1979); Okla. Stat. Ann. Tit. 40, § 2-410 (West Supp. 1980-81); Pa. Stat. Ann. Tit. 43, § 802(d) (Purdon 1964); S.D. Comp. Laws Ann. § 61-6-19 (1978); Utah Code Ann. § 35-4-5(d) (1974); Vt. Stat. Ann. Tit. 21, § 1324 (1978); Wash. Rev. Code § 50,20,090 (1979); W. Va, Code § 21A-6-3(4) (Supp. 1980); Wyo. Stat. § 27-3-106(d) (i) (1977).

[79] *See* Inter-Island Resorts, Ltd. v. Akahane, 46 Haw. 140, 377 P.2d 715 (1962).

[80] *See, e.g.,* Magner v. Kinney, 141 Neb. 122, 2 N.W.2d 689 (1942).

thus grant the striking employees unemployment compensation.[81] It should be emphasized that no exact formula is available to determine what is sufficient to constitute a work stoppage during a strike. Rather, the case law of a state must be examined to find the test applied in that state.

The numerous other issues involving unemployment compensation and strikers tend to be resolved on a state-by-state basis, by state statute or judicial construction. Thus, in some states, employer lockouts are treated the same as other labor disputes; in other states, lockouts are found to represent an involuntary disemployment of employees (even though the lockouts are precipitated by economic demands of employees) and therefore do not disqualify employees from unemployment compensation benefits. Similarly, jurisdictions differ in deciding whether sympathy strikers may be denied unemployment compensation. Various courts focus on whether the employees' refusal to cross a picket line was based on union solidarity (in which case no benefits are granted) or on a real fear of bodily injury (in which case benefits are granted.)[82]

Welfare and Food Stamps

Besides unemployment compensation benefits, strikers are often eligible for various welfare and relief funds, especially aid to dependent children and general welfare. Such funds have been found to have had a substantial influence, particularly on the ability of unions and employees to maintain strikes. The AFL-CIO, through its Department of Community Services, and other unions promote relationships and systems that facilitate the efforts of strikers to obtain welfare services and payment.[83] In addition, the strong participation of unions in community chest programs facilitates their access to private charities during strikes.

Food stamps were a prime source of striker funding until October 1981. Prior to that time, striking workers were permitted to be certified as eligible for stamps if the then liberal Food Stamp Act's income and asset requirements were met, and if the striker registered with the pertinent state employment service for available employment.[84]

All this changed on October 1, 1981, when the Reconciliation Act, signed by President Reagan on August 13, 1981, became law.[85] Section 1008 of this Act prohibits a householder from receiving an increased

---

[81] *See, e.g.,* Meadow Gold Dairies v. Wiig, 50 Haw. 225, 437 P.2d 317 (1968).

[82] *Cf.* Am. Brake Store Co. v. Annunzio, 405 Ill. 44, 90 N.E.2d 83 (1950) *with* Speagle v. United States Steel Corp., 268 Ala. 3, 105 So.2d 717 (1958).

[83] *See generally* A.J. THIEBLOT, JR., and R.M. COWIN, WELFARE AND STRIKES (1972).

[84] *Ibid.*

[85] Pub. L. No. 97-35.

allotment of food stamps "as a result of a decrease in the income of a striking member or members of the household."[86] To effectuate this change, the U.S. Department of Agriculture has issued interim regulations, which provide that food stamps will now be denied to households containing a striking member who is not exempt from the program's work registration requirements unless the household can show that, immediately prior to the strike, it would have been eligible or was receiving food stamps. A striking member is defined by the regulations as

> anyone involved in a strike or concerted stoppage of work by employees [including a stoppage by reason of the expiration of a collective bargaining agreement] and any concerted slowdown or other concerted interruption of operations by employees.[87]

WAGE AND HOUR LAWS AND THEIR APPLICATION

An employer's FLSA obligations continue during a labor dispute. Managerial employees who perform nonmanagerial work during such a dispute can lose their FLSA exempt status and become covered by the Act's overtime and other provisions. The applicable standard for deciding whether a given managerial employee loses his exempt status will turn on whether the employee is a "long test" or "short test" managerial employee. Executive employees, however, will, as a rule, retain their exempt status regardless of the kind of work they perform, for at least the initial stages of a strike.[88]

An employer's obligation to pay employees for overtime worked during a strike or lockout is the same as during normal operations. A possible wage-and-hour implication of strike operation is that managerial employees who normally are exempt from the FLSA provisions may lose the exemption if they start performing functions usually performed by regular employees covered by the FLSA. In section 213(a)(1) of the FLSA, Congress has provided that the Act's provisions do not apply to "any employee employed in a bona fide executive, administrative, or professional capacity . . . ."[89] The United States Department of Labor in turn has promulgated regulations that set forth the standards for determining whether given individuals fall into one of the managerial categories.

The Department of Labor formerly had two types of tests for determining whether an employee has exempt managerial status: "long tests"

---

[86] *Id.*, §1008.
[87] 46 FED. REG. No. 172, 44,712 (1981).
[88] 29 C.F.R. § 541.109 (a)(1979).
[89] 29 C.F.R. § 541.109 (a)(1979).

and "short tests." The two tests applied distinctly different standards for qualifying for FLSA exempt status and for losing such status.

The courts, however, have thrown out the "short tests" because they were illegally promulgated.[90] The Department of Labor has not proposed a new set of tests, and because of the antiregulation attitude of the Reagan Administration, the Department does not foresee issuing new regulations in the area. Therefore, at present, a company operating during a strike need only be concerned with the "long test."

Under the long tests, employees can earn less than $250 per week (they must earn more than $155 per week) and still qualify for managerial FLSA exempt status as long as certain other, more comprehensive requirements are satisfied.[91]

If a managerial employee qualifies for exempt status under a long test, then that test is used to determine how exempt status may be lost. If a long-test managerial employee spends more than 20 percent of his time in a given workweek performing nonexempt work, that employee's FLSA exempt status is lost.[92] Long-test managerial employees working in retail or service establishments must spend over 40 percent of their work hours in a given week doing nonexempt work before losing their exempt managerial status.[93]

All managerial employees found to be exempt from FLSA requirements because they are "executives" (as opposed to being exempt because they are "administrators" or "professionals") fall under a special Department of Labor regulation that states in part: "A bona fide executive who performs work of a normally nonexempt nature on rare occasions because of the existence of a real emergency will not, because of the performance of such emergency work, lose the exemption."[94] The Department of Labor views at least the first week after a strike begins as an "emergency" period within the ambit of the regulation.[95] Thus, for at least one week after a strike begins, employers can use "executives" in nonexempt positions without incurring possible overtime obligations to said "executives."

ANTISTRIKEBREAKING LAWS AND THE DECISION TO OPERATE

Both the federal government and certain states restrict the hiring of replacements for striking workers. The relevant laws are not onerous

---

[90] *See generally* Marshall v. Western Union Tel. Co., 621 F.2d 1246, 1252 (3d Cir. 1980).

[91] *See* 29 C.F.R. §§ 541.1(a)-(e), §§ 541.2(a)-(e), §§ 541.3(a)-(e) (1979).

[92] *See* 29 C.F.R. § 541.1(e), § 541.2(d), § 541.3(d) (1979).

[93] *Id.*

[94] 29 C.F.R. § 541.109(a) (1979).

[95] Brennan v. Western Union Telegraph Co., 561 F.2d 477, 484 (3d Cir. 1977), *cert. denied*, 434 U.S. 1063 (1978).

and should have little practical impact on successful operation of a facility. Nevertheless, care must be taken, for a company could unintentionally violate one of the laws. The intent of the laws in this area essentially is to prevent the use of professional strikebreakers.

The federal law covering this subject is the Byrnes Act.[96] The Act provides:

> Whoever willfully transports in interstate or foreign commerce any person who is employed or is to be employed for the purpose of obstructing or interfering by force or threats with (1) peaceful picketing by employees during any labor controversy affecting wages, hours, or conditions of labor, or (2) the exercise by employees of any of the rights of self-organization or collective bargaining; or
>
> Whoever is knowingly transported or travels in interstate or foreign commerce for any of the purposes enumerated in this section—
>
> Shall be fined not more than $5,000 or imprisoned not more than two years, or both.

In short, employers should *not* under *any circumstances* hire employees from another state to interfere forcibly or by threats with the right of employees to strike.

The state laws limiting an employer's right to replace striking workers generally go well beyond the Byrnes Act. Such state statutes are modeled on a proposed statute formulated by the International Typographical Union in 1960. Although the precise language of the various state laws differs, the general thrust of such statutory provisions is to prevent employers involved in a strike, lockout, or labor dispute from (1) hiring replacements through the aid of third parties not "directly involved" in the labor dispute; (2) recruiting or importing replacements from outside the given state; or (3) hiring "professional strikebreakers," or persons who have "customarily and repeatedly" worked or offered to work in place of employees involved in a strike.[97]

Legally, these state acts appear to conflict directly with the right employers have under the NLRA to replace employees and operate during strikes. The constitutionality of such state antistrikebreaking statutes is questionable. Federal labor laws have been held to preempt state legislation dealing with the same matters.[98] Indeed, in the most recent litigation involving such a statute, a New Jersey Superior Court judge ruled that state's antistrikebreaking law to be unconstitutional on the grounds that the NLRA preempted state regulation of the matter.[99] The various state antistrikebreaking statutes also are probably

---

[96] 18 U.S.C. § 1231 (1966).

[97] *See* Comment, *Anti-Strikebreaking Legislation—The Effect and Validity of State Imposed Criminal Sanctions,* 115 U. PA. L. REV. 190, 191 (1966).

[98] San Diego Building Trades Council v. Garmon, 359 U.S. 236 (1959).

[99] Chamber of Commerce v. State of New Jersey, _____ N.J. Super. _____ (June 13, 1980) (Marzulli, J.) (unpublished opinion).

open to attack on a variety of other constitutional grounds (e.g., first amendment and constitutional right to travel, in addition to the preemption doctrine).

Federal labor law, however, does not preempt all state regulation of labor-management relations. States may regulate activity that is only a peripheral concern of the NLRA, or may regulate conduct that "is deeply rooted in local feeling and responsibility."[100] Thus, although state regulation of the hiring of strike replacements, a matter that is at the core of conduct subject to federal labor law, may be preempted, states may lawfully regulate strike violence or other matters that are of great local concern.

THE IMPACT OF STATE LICENSING LAWS

Although frequently overlooked, state licensing laws may profoundly affect the ability of a company to successfully operate during a strike. The operation of nearly all modern businesses requires the use of certain technical skills. Nearly all states license individuals who practice those skills. For example, in Connecticut, electricians and plumbers, among other individuals, cannot "engage in, practice or offer to perform" work unless they are properly licensed pursuant to state law.[101] Such laws are strongly promoted by unions, particularly as a means of limiting the use of strikebreakers.[102]

The ramifications of such laws on employers attempting to operate during a strike are obvious. If an employer needs skilled electricians to maintain his equipment properly, for example, the employer may lawfully use only properly licensed electricians. Similarly, boiler operators are required by law to run a power plant, but they also must be licensed by the state. In Atlantic City, New Jersey, all employees in the casinos must be licensed by the state. During a strike, properly licensed individuals may be difficult for an employer to find, and even if they are found, the employer may have trouble convincing such persons to cross a picket line to come to work. An employer may be unable to operate successfully because of an inability to obtain the needed skills. If an employer attempts to use unlicensed personnel, it could face liability.

INJUNCTIVE RELIEF AND ITS APPLICATION

As discussed in subsequent chapters, an important right provided to employers during a labor dispute is the availability of injunctive relief

---

[100] San Diego Building Trades Council v. Garmon, 359 U.S. 236, 243-44 (1959).

[101] Conn. Gen. Stat. Ann. § 203-34 (Supp. 1980).

[102] *See* H.R. NORTHRUP *and* G.F. BLOOM, ECONOMICS OF LABOR RELATIONS 233-34 (9th ed. 1981).

against violent, intimidating, or coercive conduct by striking employees. Although the steps to be taken in preparation for such actions are discussed later, certain important legal concepts are mentioned here that should be known prior to implementing a decision to operate a facility during a strike.

An employer may bring an action for an injunction against violent, intimidating, or coercive conduct by striking employees in federal or state court and may request the NLRB to seek such relief. Because of the restrictions of the Norris-LaGuardia Act[103] and the problems involved in having the NLRB seek injunctions, federal action generally is avoided except in specific circumstances. Instead, employers normally seek relief in the state courts. Obviously the laws of each state vary, but certain generalizations can be made.

State Court Injunctions

State law usually forbids violent, intimidating, or coercive conduct by employees engaged in an otherwise lawful strike.[104] Examples of illegal conduct include mass picketing, blocking of ingress or egress, violence or threats of violence against customers or nonstriking employees, and interfering with common carriers.

Issuance of an injunction turns on the specific facts of each case, and an employer must show that the misconduct it seeks to prohibit has occurred, that the misconduct is likely to recur if the court does not prohibit it, and that the employer will suffer irreparable damage if the misconduct does recur. Moreover, the scope and nature of any injunction issued will depend on the strength of the evidence presented. Thus, an employer must adopt procedures for ensuring that all evidence of misconduct is gathered, preserved, and put in the proper form for subsequent evaluation and presentation in court.

Care must be taken in collecting and preserving evidence for purposes of obtaining an injunction. As explained above, economic strikes are protected activity under the NLRA, and an employer who interferes with, restrains, or coerces employees engaged in such a strike is guilty of an unfair labor practice under section 8(a)(1) of the Act.[105] Thus, unless proper justification is shown, photographing or otherwise monitoring strikers engaged in picketing may be held to constitute illegal interference and coercion of employees in their right to strike.[106]

---

[103] 29 U.S.C. § 101 *et seq.* (1973).

[104] *See, e.g.,* Kaplan's Fruit & Produce Co. v. Superior Court, 26 Cal. 3d 60, 160 Cal. Rptr. 745 (1979).

[105] 29 U.S.C. § 158(a)(1) (1973).

[106] *See* Puritana Mfr. Corp., 159 N.L.R.B. 518, 519 n.2 (1966).

Proper justification for employer picket line surveillance exists, however, if the employer is engaged in surveillance for the purpose of gathering evidence in order to obtain an injunction to halt unlawful strike activity.[107] If no picket line violence, mass picketing, or other unlawful strike activity has yet occurred, the employer must be able to present at least some objective evidence to substantiate that it had reason to anticipate violence or other unlawful strike activity. The employer may offer, for example, evidence of unlawful conduct in prior strikes conducted by the union.

The decision to seek an injunction should be carefully considered. In this regard, management and its counsel should evaluate the probable effectiveness of an injunction in controlling the misconduct that is occurring and the strength of the evidence that can be presented.

Injunctions can contain general prohibitions against mass picketing, violence, blocking access, making threats, or other unlawful conduct. They may also include specific restrictions as to the manner, timing, and other conditions under which picketing may be conducted. For example, when mass picketing and consequent blocking of access to an employer's premises have been shown, courts often have limited the number of pickets.[108] Specific restrictions tend to be more effective than general prohibitions because violations of them are easier to prove and because they tend to reduce the potential for disruptive conduct.

Injunctions are most effective in controlling picket-related misconduct occurring near the facility involved. Even then, an injunction's effectiveness will depend largely upon whether it contains specific restrictions on the number, spacing, and location of pickets, or simply contains general prohibitions against such conduct as blocking access and threats of violence; and second, whether the local or state police will enforce its provisions or, for political reasons, decline to do so.

Injunctions are least effective in controlling misconduct away from the plant site, such as threatening telephone calls and the following of customers and nonstriking employees, and covert misconduct near the plant, such as sabotage.

Unions or striking employees may choose not to obey an injunction, whatever its terms. If that occurs, the employer must decide whether to attempt to enforce the injunction through contempt procedures. Failure to enforce the injunction may make it more difficult to secure similar relief at some other time.

---

[107] *See* Excavation-Construction, Inc., 248 N.L.R.B. 649 (1980).

[108] *See, e.g.,* International Molders and Allied Workers Union, Local 164 v. Superior Court, 70 Cal. App.3d 395, 406, 138 Cal. Rptr. 794, 800 (1977).

Federal Court Injunctions

Although employers generally will not resort to federal court when seeking injunctive relief during an economic strike, a federal court will generally be the forum for an action to enjoin strikes in violation of a collective bargaining agreement. Federal courts might also be called on to decide the propriety of granting injunctive relief in certain unfair labor practice cases that arise during a labor dispute.

The Norris-LaGuardia Act of 1932 embodied a congressional policy against the intervention of federal courts in labor disputes. Passage of the Act represented the culmination of a bitter political, social, and economic controversy extending over half a century. Although federal courts can enjoin mass picketing and violence, the obstacles generally imposed by the Norris-LaGuardia Act lead employers to choose other forums. Thus, actions to enjoin such conduct should be focused in state courts.

On the other hand, actions to enjoin strikes in violation of a collective bargaining agreement will usually be maintained in federal court. In *Boys Markets, Inc. v. Retail Clerks' Union, Local 770*,[109] the Supreme Court accommodated the provisions of the Norris-LaGuardia Act to the provisions of section 301 of the Labor Management Relations Act and held that a federal court could enjoin a strike over a grievance that the parties are bound to arbitrate. *Boys Markets* presupposes the existence of a collective bargaining agreement with a mandatory grievance and/or arbitration procedure.

After *Boys Markets* was decided, a major area of controversy developed over whether injunctive relief was appropriate in the sympathy strike situation, in which employees honor the picket line of another union. Some courts held that the issue of whether employees may honor a picket line is an arbitral dispute, and therefore, injunctive relief like that of *Boys Markets* is appropriate.[110] Taking a narrower construction, other courts held that such strikes are not "over a grievance" and injunctive relief is inappropriate.[111] This dispute was settled by the Supreme Court in *Buffalo Forge Co. v. United Steelworkers of America*.[112]

In *Buffalo Forge,* a majority of the Court held that injunctive relief was not appropriate in sympathy strike situations. Although holding

---

[109] 398 U.S. 235 (1970).

[110] *See, e.g.,* Monongahela Power Co. v. Local 2332, IBEW, 484 F.2d 1209 (4th Cir. 1973).

[111] *See, e.g.,* Amstar Corp. v. Amalgamated Meat Cutters & Butcher Workmen, 468 F.2d 1372 (5th Cir. 1972).

[112] 428 U.S. 397 (1976). The Supreme Court will have an opportunity to reconsider Buffalo Forge in October, 1981, when it hears Jacksonville Bulk Terminals, Inc. v. International Longshoremen's Association, *cert. granted,* 101 S.Ct. 1737 (1981) (No. 80-1045).

that the issue of whether such strikes violate the terms of a no-strike clause in a collective bargaining agreement was arbitral, the Court nonetheless found that *Boys Markets* was not controlling.

The *Buffalo Forge* decision presents certain practical issues to employers who are considering operating during a strike. If the facility includes other bargaining units whose agreements have not expired at the time of the strike, employees in those units might honor picket lines, despite a no-strike clause, and the employer may be unable to obtain immediate injunctive relief. To secure relief in such a situation, an employer would have to take certain steps.

First, the employer would need to seek arbitration of the issue of whether honoring the picket line violated the collective bargaining agreement. The negotiation of an expedited arbitration clause affords a vehicle to secure an early arbitral determination. Without such a clause, problems are posed in securing a timely arbitral resolution. Once an award is issued, it can be enforced, and injunctive relief secured.[113] Thus, an employer that contemplates operating during a strike should carefully analyze its collective bargaining agreements with other bargaining units at the facility in question to ascertain the type of relief available in the event of a sympathy strike, and how such relief can best be obtained.

Injunctive relief may also be sought by the NLRB against secondary picketing when the Board has reasonable cause to believe that such picketing violates the NLRA. Section 8(b)(4) of the Act[114] prohibits unions from engaging in secondary boycotts. Of particular importance during strikes is the establishment of reserved gates to enable certain work to continue to be performed by employees of other employers. Care needs to be taken to ensure that the conditions for the establishment of such gates have been satisfied. This should be analyzed by counsel.

TORT REMEDIES FOR STRIKE VIOLENCE

Recent case law suggests that the common-law principles of tort law may be utilized to ameliorate the impact of strike violence. Courts have held that individuals subjected to union violence during a strike may bring an action under state tort law against the individuals committing such violence.

A recent example was the case in which an Arkansas state court

---

[113] *See generally* Textile Workers Union v. Lincoln Mills, 353 U.S. 448 (1957). For a critical analysis of NLRB and judicial policies in such matters, *see* T.R. HAGGARD, *Picket Line and Strike Violence as Grounds for Discharge*, 18 HOUSTON L. REV. 423 (1981).

[114] 29 U.S.C. § 158(b)(4) (1973).

awarded the plaintiffs $250,000 in damages on the basis that strike violence constituted a tortious intentional infliction of emotional distress.[115] The court concluded that the union-member defendants in the case had engaged in a "deliberate, outrageous, malicious campaign to abuse, threaten and harass the plaintiffs." Thus, state court tort actions may be one additional way to combat strike violence.

FEDERAL STATUTORY REMEDIES FOR STRIKE VIOLENCE

The common view has been that union and employee-initiated violence during a lawful strike in furtherance of legitimate collective bargaining demands is not subject to federal prosecution because the Supreme Court in *United States v. Enmons*[116] ruled that such activity is not covered by the Hobbs Act[117] prohibition against extortions. Recently, however, courts have found union-initiated violence during strikes to violate other federal statutes.

One union was found to have violated the Travel Act[118] and the Racketeer Influenced and Corrupt Organization Act[119] by using explosives to damage trucks in interstate commerce, by crossing state lines to commit arson on the struck company's trucks, and by conspiring to conduct union affairs (an enterprise) through a pattern of racketeering (the various violent acts).[120] The Ninth Circuit Court concluded that *Emmons* was narrowly focused on the Hobbs Act so as not to turn minor picket line violence into federal crimes. Moreover, the circuit court continued, in *Emmons,* the Supreme Court did not intend to exempt unions committing serious violence from all federal criminal liability.

In a different case,[121] all of the unions in an area building trades council were enjoined and assessed damages for a violent mob action against a nonunion employer on a construction site under the Civil Rights Act of 1871 (the Ku Klux Klan Act).[122] The holding of the court turned on the fact that the violence was not associated with any ongoing legitimate labor dispute (the unions were not involved in a dispute over recognition). Nevertheless, this ruling suggests other means to ameliorate the impact of strike violence.

---

[115] Boyd v. Russell, No. 78-488 (Cir. Ct. Garland Cty, Ark., July 7, 1980).

[116] 410 U.S. 396 (1973). *See generally* T.R. HAGGARD, *Labor Violence: The Inadequate Response of the Federal Anti-Extortion Statutes,* 59 NCB L. REV. 859 (1980).

[117] 18 U.S.C. § 1951(b)(2).

[118] 18 U.S.C. § 1952.

[119] 18 U.S.C. § 1962(d).

[120] United States v. Thordarson, 646 F.2d 1323 (9th Cir. 1981), *cert. denied,* 50 U.S.L.W. 3396, No. 81-643 (Nov. 16, 1981).

[121] Scott v. Moore, 640 F.2d 708 (5th Cir. 1981).

[122] 42 U.S.C. § 1985(3).

GOVERNMENTAL REGULATORY AGENCY ACTION

The explosion of government regulation of the workplace over the past twenty years has given unions new weapons in their attempts to diminish the ability of employers to operate during a strike. Experience has shown that unions have placed pressure on federal, state, and local regulatory agencies during strikes. Although such agencies may not take action beyond that prescribed by specific statutes or regulations, the agencies may focus their enforcement attention on a specific business or plant operating during a strike. Although legal considerations may be important in such situations, the practical considerations may be of greater concern. Through the ability to monitor production activity, the agencies may interfere with how the plant is operated and may even affect the level of operation.[123]

In recent strike situations unions have, for example, attempted to utilize the Occupational Safety and Health Administration (OSHA) as a vehicle to impede operation, particularly during the Carter Administration. During a strike at a British Petroleum refinery, the company was faced with having the Department of Labor conduct an investigation of employee complaints even though the employees who filed the complaints were participating in the strike.[124]

Legal questions are raised by an OSHA investigation of employee complaints during a strike. The OSHA *Field Operations Manual* specifically allows for investigations in the midst of a labor dispute.[125] Investigations during a strike, however, may move the government from the neutral role it is expected to maintain during a labor dispute.[126]

An employer is not defenseless against OSHA inspections during a strike. The government is not free to inspect at will. Specifically, an employer may challenge a proposed inspection in a search warrant proceeding. A company may argue that OSHA has insufficient grounds to establish the probability of a violation and that the inspection is not part of a comprehensive administrative plan, thus the agency fails to satisfy the constitutional fourth amendment requirement for a

---

[123] *See, e.g.,* BP Oil, Inc. v. Marshall, 509 F. Supp. 802 (E.D. Pa. 1981).

[124] *Id.*

[125] The *Field Operations Manual* provides that: "Plants or establishments may be inspected regardless of the existence of labor disputes involving work stoppage, strikes, or picketing. . . . The [compliance safety and health officer] must take great care to avoid involvement in the dispute while at the same time carrying out his responsibilities in determining whether the employer is complying with the Act." Chapter V(D)(1)(g).

[126] Regarding inspections during a strike, the *Field Operations Manual* states that "[t]he [compliance safety and health officer] should avoid injecting himself in labor relations disputes either between a recognized union and the employer or between two unions competing for bargaining rights." Chapter V(D)(4)(a).

warrant.[127] In addition, an employer may argue that the employee's complaint underlying the application for a warrant fails to conform to section 8(f) of the Occupational Safety and Health Act by being, for example, insufficiently specific or insufficiently reliable.[128] Finally, even if a warrant is issued, the employer may be able to limit the scope of the inspection so that it reasonably relates to the alleged violations.[129] The outcome of an employer challenge, of course, turns on the facts of each case. Nevertheless, as with the other tactics used by striking employees to disrupt operation, an employer has weapons available to counter the employees' actions.

A second legal problem raised by an OSHA investigation during a strike concerns the rights of striking employees to actively participate in the inspection. Although the law gives employees an opportunity to accompany a compliance safety and health officer during an inspection of a workplace,[130] the law is unclear concerning a striking employee's right to accompany the officer on such an inspection. A recent United States District Court decision holding that an employer may exclude a striking employee fails to settle the law.[131]

Intervention by OSHA as a result of union prompting can lead to large fines and penalties even after a strike has ended. In one recent situation, a union worked with OSHA once a strike had ended to bring about a major wall-to-wall inspection culminating in fines of over $700,000 and proposed abatement procedures that would have been extremely costly to implement. The union met with OSHA officials prior to the wall-to-wall inspection and provided OSHA with a list of safety complaints that the union that solicited from its members. When the company started to litigate, OSHA backed down and settled for minor fines and little company action.

Other branches of government may also move to pressure an employer attempting to operate during a strike. State health officials inspected a struck food processor once a week for the duration of a several-month strike. During normal operations such inspections occurred monthly at the most, and usually only two to three times a year. In the early 1960s, the Civil Aeronautics Board intervened in a strike-related dispute between Southern Airlines and the pilots' union by

---

[127] *See* Marshall v. Barlow's, Inc., 436 U.S. 307 (1978).

[128] 29 U.S.C. § 657(f).

[129] Marshall v. North American Car Co., 626 F.2d 320 (3d Cir. 1980).

[130] 29 U.S.C. § 657(e); 29 C.F.R. § 1903.8(a), (b).

[131] Amoco Oil Co. v. Marshall, 496 F. Supp. 1234 (S.D. Tex. 1980). The court indicated that the implementing regulations for the Occupational Safety and Health Act may provide a means to circumvent the court's holding. *See* n.16. Thus, the practical significance of this decision may be limited, even if it accurately interprets the law.

threatening to rescind the airlines' operating license if the company did not change its position.

Companies with federal contracts also may be subject to special pressures as a result of those contracts. Unless the contracts specifically allow for time delays because of labor disruptions, a company could find itself in breach of contract. Including delay clauses in their contracts enables companies to counter government pressure. Even if legally protected, labor disputes may provide an excuse to review existing contracts, as the Department of Defense did with Lockheed Aircraft in 1962, or consider more closely pending contracts bids. Thus, a company planning to operate during a strike faces a myriad of possible pressures from governmental agencies trying to impede operation, particularly when a prounion administration is in power.

SUMMARY

This chapter illustrates the pervasive role of the law during labor disputes. Employers that consider and implement a decision to operate during a strike should be cognizant of their legal obligations and the impact these obligations have on their decision. Subsequent chapters illustrate how these considerations interact with a decision to operate.

CHAPTER III

The Decision to Operate

The decision to operate a plant has both institutional and economic overtones. The literature of labor relations has tended to stress the institutional implications of a decision to operate and to question the motives of employers in making that decision. Thus, the Independent Study Group, which, in principle, gave its unqualified support to the right of employers to operate during strikes, also felt compelled, in practice, to urge employers not to avail themselves of that right:

> Violence does erupt occasionally, however, usually where the union's continued existence is threatened by an employer's effort to operate his plant during a strike. Such a move on the part of an employer challenges the union's status as exclusive bargaining agent for workers in the unit and thereby transforms the strike from an incident in a longterm bargaining relationship to a war for survival. The desire to avoid violence and to maintain a working spirit between labor and management, along with employer respect for union strength, and for the achievements of collective bargaining, has led most employers not to attempt back-to-work movements during a strike.[1]

There is little doubt that a decision to operate during a strike may be based primarily on institutional considerations and implemented with the goal of breaking a union. The "back-to-work movement" model of plant operation on which the Independent Study Group focused its attention is consistent with an institutional view of plant operation because it directly challenges the "union's continued existence." More recently, a direct challenge to union power has been cited as an integral part of "conflict" relationships:

> In the conflict relation, management strongly opposes the very existence of the union. It does more or less everything it can to prevent or eliminate unionization. . . . If a union manages to organize a plant despite such efforts, management will deal with it because it must. But it will make no secret of its desire to eliminate the union. . . . If there is a strike, management will try to break the union as well as the strike.[2]

---

[1] COMMITTEE FOR ECONOMIC DEVELOPMENT, THE PUBLIC INTEREST IN NATIONAL LABOR POLICY 88 (1961).

[2] E. EDWARD HERMAN AND ALFRED KUHN, COLLECTIVE BARGAINING AND LABOR RELATIONS 79 (1981).

It is also possible that a decision to operate can be motivated solely by economic considerations and serve only to permit a firm to take rather than break a strike. This possibility has not been explicitly recognized in the literature, but deserves consideration in light of economic developments over the past decade—developments that have greatly increased the cost to employers of nonoperation and have decreased their "respect for union strength, and for the achievements of collective bargaining." The growth of foreign and domestic non-union competition in many industries has raised the cost of strikes to management in terms of both loss of sales in the short run and market share in the long run.[3] In addition, increasing union recourse to such power tactics as coalition bargaining and selective strikes, together with the growing ability of employees to withstand long strikes, raises the price paid at the bargaining table and in the market by manage-ment in taking a strike.[4] Of course, any firm operating simply to cut its strike losses would do so in a manner that would not threaten the jobs of striking workers or the status of the striking union.

The third possibility is that a decision to operate is based on both economic and institutional considerations and designed both to cut losses and to gain power. This possibility has been recognized in the literature as an element in "power bargaining" in which management does not feel constrained "to avoid violence and to maintain a working spirit between labor and management." Power bargaining has been characterized, in part, as follows:

> The difference between conflict and power bargaining is roughly that between cold war and peaceful but competitive coexistence. As in conflict relations, management also sees the union as an undesirable obstruction be-tween itself and its employees. But it concludes that the union is there to stay and ceases open attempts to destroy [it]. . . . Management will try to keep the union weak and defensive. . . . Although management would not hire professional strikebreakers, it will try to operate during a strike, possibly hire new employees to replace strikers, and appeal to union members over the heads of their leaders to return to work or accept a management-proposed contract.[5]

The questions of "why" and "how" firms decide to attempt plant operation are not easy to answer. The only reasonably objective basis for attempting to answer these questions is a review of the origins

---

[3] For a statement of some of the economic reasons that management has lost respect for union strength and for the achievements of collective bargaining, *see* Peter J. Pestillo, *Learning to Live Without the Union, in* PROCEEDINGS OF THE THIRTY-FIRST ANNUAL MEETING, INDUSTRIAL RELATIONS RESEARCH ASSOCIATION 2,233-39 (1979).

[4] For a discussion of the broader power implications of these developments, *see* George H. Hilderbrand, *Bargaining Structure and Relative Power, in* COLLECTIVE BARGAINING: SURVIVAL IN THE '70'S? 10-23 (R. Rowan ed. 1972).

[5] HERMAN *and* KUHN, *supra.*

and evolutions of the policies and practices of firms that have taken the difficult and unpopular step of operating production facilities during strikes. This review will describe both the role and limits of plant operation as a management power asset in collective bargaining.

CORPORATE POLICY

All of the companies studied had elaborate formal policies and procedures to guide plant management in the handling of a strike threat or a strike in the course of contract negotiations. None of these formal policies directed the operation of plants during strikes. All, however, explicitly recognized operation as a legitimate option open to plant management should business conditions warrant. For example, the strike manual of one of the firms indicated that the following factors should be considered in "management decisions in the face of a strike threat":

1. *The Company's Inventory Position*

    a. How many months' supply of the most important products is available in accessible places?

    b. Is it possible to move finished products to an accessible place before or after the strike begins?

2. *Production Capability*

    Will it be possible or economically feasible to produce critical items:

    a. In other plants of the company?

    b. By salaried personnel?

    c. By replacements for striking workers?

    d. By other firms?

3. *Market Position of the Company*

    What will be the consequence of having products off the market for a period of time?

The formal policies of all the firms stressed the prospect of a serious loss of sales and particularly market position as a key factor in the decision to operate. The policies of most companies conditioned the decision to operate not only on economic necessity but also on institutional feasibility. Thus, the factors to be considered in the decision to maintain production typically included:

1. How critical is the company's inventory position? Would it be possible to forego production for a month to six weeks without suffering serious losses in sales and market position?

2. What is the attitude of local government officials? Can the company expect the cooperation and protection it may need if it attempts to maintain production? Will it be possible to obtain a court injunction should illegal strike activity occur?

3. Will a sufficient number of competent personnel be available for scheduled operations from among the salaried group, together with hourly employees who elect to work and newly hired replacements?

4. Will the local union resort to every means possible to prevent the plant from operating? How much backing is the international union and the rest of the labor movement likely to give if the local union attempts to prevent plant operation?

5. Will common carriers and local delivery drivers be willing to cross a picket line? Will company drivers with leased equipment be able to handle the movement of goods in and out of the plant?

Overall, the formal policies of the firms studied suggest that plant operation is an option to be used when (1) there is a high risk of loss of market position in the event of nonoperation, and (2) there is a high probability of success in the event of operation. For a plant to have a high probability of successful operation, two conditions must be met: (1) a reasonable assurance of an adequate supply of labor to man the plant (the "fear of failure"), and (2) a reasonable assurance that the striking union's response to operation will be limited or manageable (the "fear of confrontation"). One approach to plant operation that offers the greatest hope on both counts is to rely exclusively on managerial and supervisory personnel in manning a struck facility. This is the basic policy of virtually all of the firms studied.

The policies of all of the firms were basically silent on whether short-run or long-run tactical advantage in collective bargaining is a consideration in a decision to operate. The obvious and perhaps intended implication of this silence is that operation, as a matter of policy, is intended to serve only as a defensive economic weapon. The fact that a high probability of success is one of the conditions for use of that weapon, however, suggests that institutional as well as economic considerations have influenced corporate policy on operation. A review of the origins of such policy clearly confirms that suspicion.

The Origins of Corporate Policy

The plant operation policies of all the firms studied are very different today than they were twenty years ago when, for all intents and purposes, the firms pursued policies of nonoperation. A few of the firms could recall scattered instances of ad hoc plant operation prior to 1960, but in all but one case these were isolated, idiosyncratic events. In that exceptional case, the firm asserted that it had first utilized plant operation as a basic strategic option in 1948 and has continued to do so ever since. That company also admitted, however, that its true commitment to a policy of operating during strikes was not tested until the 1960s. Another firm reported a few cases of partial operation of small plants during the 1950s, but it too admitted that its real commitment to operation as a strategic option did not come until the 1960s. Finally, a third company reported that some of its divisions were believed to have operated plants during strikes as early as the late 1940s, but also reported that most such activity has taken place since 1970.

Changes in the plant operation policies of the firms studied were concentrated in two periods: the early 1960s and the early 1970s. Both of these periods were characterized by relatively low rates of economic growth in comparison with the record of the preceding decade. Both also were periods of growing competition for customers in most product markets with little prospect of an early return to the sellers' markets that had prevailed in previous years. The result was a substantial increase in the potential costs of nonoperation in terms of market position, a development that had to raise questions regarding the virtue of a policy of nonoperation in the minds of any number of managements. The same may well be the case today inasmuch as economic conditions and prospects in the early 1980s bear a striking resemblance to those of the early 1960s and 1970s, making conditions right for yet another wave of change in policies on plant operation.

About one-half of the firms studied abandoned their policy or practice of nonoperation in the early 1960s. In virtually all of those cases, the decision to operate, as a matter of policy, was the product of more than growing business necessity. Specifically, that decision was part of a more basic change in labor relations philosophy and policy brought about in most cases by turnover in top management, which removed from the scene those who had decided in the 1940s to accept and possibly to encourage unionism and collective bargaining. The essence of this change in philosophy was a new determination to resist unions both in the field and at the bargaining table in an effort to contain the growth of unionism within the company.

The basic goal of these new labor relations policies was to limit the spread of organization beyond those company facilities already unionized. Those policies did not aim to eliminate unionism where it already existed, but they did aim, through greater resistance to union bargaining demands, to limit unions' gains at the bargaining table and, correspondingly, their appeal to unorganized workers.

The result was a conscious decision to pursue power bargaining in lieu of a more accommodative approach in collective bargaining. This approach included use of the plant operation option, but not some of the more drastic tactics associated with that option, such as hiring permanent replacements or encouraging back-to-work movements.

The remaining half of the firms studied altered their traditional policies of nonoperation in the early 1970s. In general, this wave of change in policies seemed to have been pragmatic rather than philosophical. Some of these firms "stumbled" into plant operation on an ad hoc basis in the 1960s and, based on that experience, recognized plant operation as a basic strategic option in subsequent negotiations. Some firms were forced into operation by the needs of a special customer or a particularly important and difficult economic issue in bargaining, and they, too, subsequently built this option into their basic labor relations policies. Several firms were targets of coalition bargaining in the late 1960s and adopted plant operation as a means to counter that union power tactic. For virtually all of these firms, plant operation was conceived basically as a defensive weapon designed to serve a narrow economic purpose.

CORPORATE PRACTICE

The relatively common formal policies governing the decision to operate among the firms studied mask some significant differences in the plant operation practices. Specifically, the practices of the firms appear to divide into four basic categories:

1. Plant operation as a secondary option to be used only in cases of compelling business need;

2. Plant operation as a selective option to be used only when and where a compelling economic or strategic case can be made;

3. Plant operation as a preferred option to be used unless a compelling case can be made against operation on the grounds of feasibility or necessity;

4. Plant operation as a paramount option to be used in all strike situations as a matter of principle.

There was no simple and obvious pattern to the way in which the firms were distributed among these four categories. Instead, that distribution appeared to reflect a combination of technological (fear of failure) and institutional (fear of confrontation) considerations in which institutional considerations often were at least as important as technological ones.

Firms for which plant operation is a less favored option typically were one of two types. First, firms requiring fairly large and/or highly skilled work forces to man their facilities (shipbuilding, computer manufacturing) generally do not make a real effort to operate during strikes unless there is a very substantial back-to-work movement among striking personnel. They may, however, attempt partial operation using salaried personnel to finish work in progress in order to meet delivery commitments to major customers. Second, firms producing consumer goods (drugs) also are reluctant to undertake operation absent some pressing and publicly justifiable business need out of concern for the possible consumer reaction to any publicity surrounding a potential confrontation with unions.

At the other end of the spectrum, firms for which plant operation is the rule rather than the exception generally are firms that face little difficulty in manning facilities using salaried personnel (oil refining, chemical manufacturing) and little prospect of an effective adverse consumer reaction to any publicity surrounding a confrontation with unions. The firms in this category also are typically very much committed to power bargaining as an offensive weapon in labor relations.

Between the two extremes, the array of firms is less easily explained. Among those firms for which plant operation is a preferred option are a number of firms for which operation is not technologically difficult, but there are also a number of firms for which this is not the case. The same is true among those firms for which plant operation is a selective option. The primary difference between the two categories rests in degree of acceptance of power bargaining as a basic managerial strategy—acceptance that appears to have been shaped as much by experience as by original intent.

The Evolution of Practice

The records of the firms studied suggest that plant operation may be addictive. There was a perceptible tendency for firms to move along the scale of plant operation practice over time as they gained experience. The result has been to move most firms more deeply into the power bargaining model of union-management relations. Thus far, however, basically none have crossed the line into the conflict model of such relations, although there are a few isolated plant situations in which that line was broached, if not breached.

Fear of Failure

The records and remarks of the firms studied clearly indicate that the fear of failure diminishes as firms gain experience in operating plants. Thus, once beyond the trauma of initial operating experience, many firms wondered why they had not tried it earlier or why other firms do not follow their example. The experience and confidence gained by most firms in early plant operation attempts encouraged virtually all to repeat and extend such attempts, and subsequent experience has done the same. The result in most firms has been a dramatic expansion of the perceived technological limits on the company's ability to operate during strikes.

The addictive effect of plant operation is most prominent among those firms that began plant operation in the early 1960s, but it is by no means confined to those firms. One firm that ventured somewhat tentatively into plant operation around 1960 now states that its policy is committed to operating during strikes. Another firm with a similar policy is now prepared to operate multiple facilities simultaneously should the need arise. Several other firms whose policies are to "operate except in extraordinary circumstances" are hard pressed to identify an exception that would qualify under this rule. One such firm has not found an exception in the last ten years. Another cited only one—an explosives plant—which it is now prepared to attempt to operate should the need arise. Finally, one company whose formal policy dates from the early 1970s and which views plant operation as a selective option reported a consistent upward trend in acceptance of this option by local plant management within the first five years.

Fear of Confrontation

The records and remarks of the firms studied also indicate that the fear of confrontation, like the fear of failure, diminishes with experience. More precisely, experience with plant operation produces a better appreciation of the potential economic (defensive) and institutional (offensive) benefits of power bargaining in general. In many cases, that appreciation has reinforced the company's willingness to risk both failure and confrontation by attempting to operate facilities that cannot be manned effectively using only company salaried personnel.

Those firms that initially viewed plant operation as an offensive as well as a defensive weapon clearly have not changed their view. The effectiveness of plant operation as an offensive weapon, however, depends on the success of the company in operating during any and all strikes. In order to meet this challenge, some firms have been forced, albeit reluctantly in most cases, to hire temporary or permanent replacements for striking workers, and at least one other has felt compelled to plan for simultaneous operation of several struck facilities in the face of an intensive union-organizing campaign.

Those firms that were drawn into plant operation primarily by defensive considerations have not been oblivious to the offensive potential of plant operation. One such firm, which began operation in response to coalition bargaining, now uses salaried employees and temporary replacements to man plants during selective/sequential lockouts. Another firm drawn into plant operation by the needs of a special customer ultimately found it necessary to hire permanent replacements to sustain operations and then could not resist the temptation to raise a question of representation—a temptation that most other firms have been careful to resist.

The fact that plant operation is a popular option for management with experience suggests that, once tried, plant operation tends to become an integral part of collective bargaining. This has been the case in the oil and telephone industries, is becoming the case in the chemical and newspaper industries, and may become the case in such new entrants to the field as the paper and hotel industries. Once used, plant operation may spread by virtue of example or force of competitive pressure, as in the oil and chemical industries. Once thus entrenched, plant operation seems unlikely to be dislodged until a new set of technological or institutional barriers to successful operation are created by either law or the ingenuity of the labor movement. No such barriers seem likely to emerge in the immediate future, but what lies beyond that limited horizon remains to be seen.

CORPORATE PLANNING

The companies studied unanimously agreed that the commitment to plant operation required detailed operating plans for each production facility. The myriad problems encountered when operating a plant under siege with an inexperienced and limited work force simply cannot be managed on an ad hoc basis. Even with the best of plans, those problems may tax management's ingenuity to the limit.

The Need to Plan

The importance of careful planning to the success of any attempt to operate has been learned the hard way by several of the firms. Those firms were ones that had been forced into attempting to operate with relatively little planning because they had failed to anticipate a strike and make provisions to meet customer needs during a strike. While most firms had been able to operate on a limited basis in such situations, none claimed any real success in those efforts. The lesson of such experience was sufficiently painful to force the firms to develop comprehensive operating plans.

In all of the firms studied, planning for possible plant operation is now a routine element in the overall process of preparing for contract negotiations. This process often begins as early as one year prior to contract expiration and is fairly well completed before negotiations open. Thus, the planning process involves anticipating all of the problems that may arise in the event of plant operation during a possible strike. Fortunately, for most of the companies studied, this rather formidable task is simplified by their ability to draw on a substantial body of accumulated experience. All that is required is an update of existing plans to reflect problems encountered previously in attempting to operate, as well as anticipation of any "new developments" likely to emerge—developments that inevitably seem to occur in every additional experience in plant operation.

The Responsibility of Planning

The basic responsibility for planning for operation during a strike rests with plant management. The crucial decisions are line decisions regarding what will be produced and how it will be produced under strike conditions. Despite this fact, substantial responsibility often is delegated to industrial relations personnel in the development of strike plans at the plant level. Once such plans are developed, they generally are subject to review by corporate industrial relations personnel and approval by top-line management. At this point, a decision might be made not to operate the plant in the event of a strike for either economic, institutional, or technological reasons.

The fact that operation requires the assumption of risk makes decisions to operate the subject of varying degrees of internal controversy. Generally, it is corporate personnel, particularly corporate industrial relations personnel, who are likely to be the "hawks" in such controversy, with the role of the "doves" being played by plant personnel, particularly plant-line personnel. These roles, however, can be and have been reversed. In one case, an industrial chemical plant had to lobby long to convince its parent corporation, primarily a producer of consumer goods, to run the risk of adverse publicity and permit the plant to operate during a strike.

The Elements of a Plan

A staggering array of policy issues and practical problems face a company contemplating plant operation. The complexity of these issues and problems is amply demonstrated by the detailed strike plans of most of the firms studied. A composite example of a strike plan or manual is provided in the appendix. Overall, such plans suggest that there are seven key areas that any strike plan should cover:

1. Production
2. Shipping and receiving
3. Maintenance
4. Industrial relations
5. Plant security
6. Communications
7. Legal representation

The "strike preparation plan and check list" of one plant addressed these seven key areas in the following terms:

1. *Production Preparation*
    a. Determine what is required to place plant in a safe (stand-by and continued production) condition in the event of a strike. Devise a takeover strategy to assure continuity of operations.
    b. Determine production plans for strike period. Determine which units can be shut down and for how long. Set priority on production needs and production runs required.
    c. Determine minimum manning requirements for each production and service department (assume twelve-hour shifts). Assign individuals to departments.
    d. Establish specific manning assignments, work schedules, and stand-by schedules. Notify employees in advance of their assignment.
    e. Determine which individuals will need special licenses or certificates to perform their assignments and ensure that such licenses are secured.
    f. Establish necessary training programs and train people prior to start of work.

2. *Supply Preparations*

   a. Develop raw material strategy based on inventories and production plans.

   b. Set up plans for in-plant storage of raw materials and finished goods. Set up outside warehousing where required.

   c. Make arrangements for delivery of raw materials and shipment of finishing products (trucks, barge and rail service) (nonunion tows). Establish a remote trans-shipping point.

   d. Establish operating supply levels and requirements, including maintenance material requirements. Check supply of personal safety equipment (goggles, hats, rubber boots, respirators).

   e. Provide work clothing (coveralls) for areas where required. Coordinate issue of personal protection equipment.

   f. Make purchasing arrangements for items specified prior to the strike (food service, sleeping accommodations, contract work). Establish delivery of vehicle fuel. Arrange for rental van for use in pick up of operating supplies. Contract for janitorial service (plantwide) during the strike.

3. *Maintenance Preparations*

   a. Review maintenance needs to ensure completion of major necessary items prior to contract expiration. Complete all outside contract work prior to contract termination date.

   b. Determine which routine maintenance work must be done for safe operation.

   c. Determine special skills or crafts needed. Determine craft help required from other company plants in addition to assignments to plant salaried personnel.

   d. Provide handtools and tool boxes for maintenance work.

   e. Establish central engineering group to handle emergency maintenance or construction work.

   f. Prepare plans (names of people or contractors) for outside contract help for major breakdowns or maintenance work beyond scope of plant personnel.

4. *Personnel Preparations*

   a. Update list of all employees' names, addresses, telephone numbers, and license numbers.

b. Establish and issue policies on pay, method of keeping track of hours worked (or held in plant), charges (if any) for food service.

c. Establish orderly procedure for notification of salaried and nonbargaining-unit employees as to their reporting for work prior to the establishment of picket lines.

d. Arrange for food and beverage service in-plant (refrigerator trucks, food supply, dishes, help in cafeteria, etc.). Assign qualified manager for food service operation or hire one from outside.

e. Arrange for sleeping accommodations. Establish designated locations for sleeping accommodations (building areas, campers, railroad sleeping cars). Rent cots, roll-away beds, blankets, pillows, etc. in advance.

f. Coordinate recreation activity for employees confined to the plant. Rent a television and provide antenna in central location. Have daily papers delivered to plant cafeteria. Establish plan for mail service to and from the plant.

g. Assure proper medical coverage in the plant at all times.

5. *Security Preparations*

a. Check and repair plant fence. Clean up and check perimeter road. Check that all no-trespassing and no-parking signs are intact.

b. Install signs establishing gate numbers for identification. Establish a construction gate and clearly mark as a construction entrance only.

c. Establish adequate, state-approved area within main plant site for temporary effluent and solid waste disposal.

d. Establish security lighting. Rent equipment for plant patrol duty. Establish patrol routes, times, plans. Make preparations for rental guards and guard dogs. Arrange for protection of barge unloading facility, main electric subsection, and other remote facilities and utility linkages.

e. Arrange for alternate telephone communications. Assign two-way radios. Check radio communication system and rent additional equipment if required. Set up CB to monitor.

f. Provide camper at main plant entrance for observation of picket line. Install observation penthouse on roof of main building and equip with TV camera and telescope.

g. Arrange training session to advise nonstrikers how to handle threats and hostile confrontations. Establish a procedure for quickly obtaining affidavits.

h. Establish a trained fire brigade and fire protection plan. Be sure equipment is in working order. Be certain all valves are properly set in the plant sprinkler system. Be certain necessary extinguishers and supplies are available.

i. Establish working relationship with state police and local law enforcement agencies. Keep them informed on potential strike and developments if a strike occurs.

6. *Communications Preparations*

a. Establish in-plant newsletter and recorded telephone messages for communication of daily news of strike-related developments.

b. Prepare letters to inform suppliers and customers of the strike or threatened strike.

c. Prepare press releases and establish that all public relations activities will be handled by one specified individual.

7. *Legal Preparations*

a. Arrange in advance for the service of a qualified local labor attorney to assist in securing injunctions and dealing with unemployment compensation problems should the need arise.

b. Determine in advance the requirements and procedures for securing and implementing an injunction.

c. Establish a system to maintain an accurate log of strike-related activities, events, photographs, etc. from the first sign of any strike activity.

The kinds of preparations called for in operating plans like the one above require substantial lead time and can be expensive to implement. For example, one company reported spending almost $10,000 for the following in its preparations to operate one relatively small plant:

1. Portable video camera and recorder

2. Four camper trailers (rental)

3. Thirty-five aluminum folding cots (rental)

4. Two color televisions (rental)

5. Forty-eight pairs of coveralls

6. Two Chevrolet Blazers (rental)

7. One backhoe (rental)

8. One freezer truck (rental)

9. Frozen food and meal supplies

10. Five diesel-powered portable lights

11. Twelve six-volt lanterns

12. One gasoline powered generator (rental)

Clearly, no firm would want to make this kind of investment if operation were going to prove unnecessary. Given uncertainty regarding the ultimate necessity of plant operation, firms may either refrain from implementing preparations to operate and hope for the best or proceed with those preparations in fear of the worst. In practice, most firms make this decision in stages as more information about the probable outcome of negotiations becomes available. In the final analysis, however, the firms studied almost invariably choose to err on the side of protecting themselves against the worst rather than hoping for the best.

Effect of Preparations on Union

The decision to proceed with preparations to operate sets in motion a series of actions that are visible to the union and constitute a signal that the company intends to operate if a strike occurs. Most firms make no attempt to mask their preparations or mute the signal they provide, and some do quite the opposite. The companies studied differed in their perceptions of the impact these signals have on the union and its bargaining posture, with their views ranging from "no effect" to a slight "softening effect." Whatever effect is felt appears to depend not on the company's intent to operate, but on the perceived ability of the company to operate successfully. If a union and its membership are not convinced that management can operate successfully in the face of a strike, preparation for operation will have little effect on the outcome of negotiations.

SUMMARY

The two major deterrents to the exercise of the right to operate are the fear of failure and the fear of confrontation. Firms that have overcome these fears have done so for varying combinations of economic (defensive) and institutional (offensive) reasons. Whatever their original motives for its use, plant operation tends to become an offensive rather than a purely defensive weapon in a power bargaining relationship. Despite the offensive character and potential of plant operation, however, it is generally not perceived or practiced by management as a weapon to eliminate unionism where it already exists. At most, plant operation is utilized to keep unions weak and defensive, particularly in their efforts to organize nonunion plants.

When the fears of failure and confrontation have been once overcome, their deterrent effect quickly weakens with experience. Thus, plant operation tends to move the parties more deeply into power bargaining relationships over time. The result is a growing challenge to unions to find ways in which to counter management's ability and willingness to operate.

The risk of failure and confrontation can never be eliminated but can be limited by careful preparation for plant operation. Such planning is routine for all firms committed to even selective exercise of the right to operate simply because experience has shown that it is easier not to operate with a plan than to operate without a plan.

CHAPTER IV

The Logistics of Operation: Manpower

The critical problem facing an employer that decides to operate during a strike is securing an adequate supply of labor to man production operations. One source of such labor—the one on which the Independent Study Group focused its attention—is members of the bargaining unit who are sufficiently disenchanted with strike action to participate in a back-to-work movement. A second source of such labor—one that has become vastly more important than disillusioned strikers in the logistics of plant operation—is salaried and other nonunion employees. Finally, an employer may seek external replacements for striking workers.

STRIKING WORKERS

Most of the companies studied based their operating plans on the assumption that a strike would be totally effective in preventing members of the bargaining unit from reporting to work. Furthermore, the overwhelming majority of the firms do little or nothing to attempt to limit the effectiveness of a strike within the bargaining unit. Specifically, most firms consciously or unconsciously have heeded the advice of the Independent Study Group to avoid the explosiveness of back-to-work movements.

This has not always been the case and is not always the case today, particularly in the operation of large, labor-intensive facilities. Although one major producer in the electrical industry did at one time operate such a facility with bargaining-unit members, successful operation was the result of some special local circumstances surrounding the union's strike call. That situation is acknowledged to have been truly unusual, and the company admits that it has not actively planned or attempted to operate that facility since, and would not barring similarly unusual circumstances. A more recent notable exception was the success of one of the nation's leading shipbuilding companies, Newport News Shipbuilding and Dry Dock Company, in operating its highly labor-intensive facility with bargaining-unit members. Once again, the circumstances surrounding the strike were unusual in that the strike occurred over union recognition at a time when legal challenges were being mounted to overturn the NLRB's certification of the striking union.

Although the companies generally did not attempt to limit the effectiveness of strikes, most companies, as a matter of formal policy, have kept their plants open for any and all bargaining-unit members who might wish to report. Few companies, however, communicated that policy to the union or employees at the time of a strike. The remainder of the companies were satisfied to have the policy on the books as a basis for responding to questions from individual employees, the press, or the government. All of the companies took steps to ensure that such questions would be answered correctly by instructing their managerial and supervisory personnel either how to answer the questions or to refer the questions to the plant industrial relations personnel.

Open-Door Policies

The existence of formal open-door policies does not mean that companies generally have sought or welcomed the return to work of individual bargaining-unit members. Virtually all of the companies studied reported that a few individuals expressed interest in reporting for work during the course of a strike, including some who were willing to stay on the job at the time the strike began. In general, the companies informally counselled them against such action, pointing out the worker's potential vulnerability to union discipline and the problems that such action might create for the worker's short-term physical and long-term social welfare. In addition, the lack of enthusiasm about individual returnees in many of the firms reflected concern about the motives and reliability of individuals choosing to return to work during a plant operation situation.

Concern over retribution against individual bargaining-unit members who cross the picket line was universal among the companies studied and was, in several cases, supported by experience ranging from social ostracism to physical violence. Concern over possible espionage against the company was somewhat less prevalent and less easily substantiated on the basis of experience, perhaps because most companies carefully assigned or closely supervised those individuals who returned to work during a strike.

Return-to-Work Movements

The lack of enthusiasm of most companies about the return of individual bargaining-unit members to work during a strike was accompanied by a similar lack of enthusiasm about larger-scale return-to-work movements. Most companies ignored the possibility of such a movement in developing their operating plan, primarily because they perceived little likelihood that a sufficiently large contingent of disgruntled strikers would emerge to provide the critical mass necessary for a successful return-to-work movement. Thus, although most firms theoretically were ready to accommodate return-to-work movements, few were practically prepared to do so.

The low probability of a successful return-to-work movement, coupled with the high probability of increased violence should such a movement occur, led most companies to assume a "hands-off" policy with respect to any sentiment among bargaining-unit members for a return to work. Indeed, a few companies actively discouraged this sentiment and encouraged dissident strikers to focus their attention instead on inducing their union to reconsider or formally vote on management's last offer. Newport News Shipbuilding and Dry Dock Company was the only clear exception to this rule. A few other firms in the sample have, in isolated cases, also abandoned their neutrality to encourage back-to-work movements as part of a broader effort to sustain operation in the face of a prolonged strike, an effort that has included the hiring of permanent replacements. Most firms, however, are satisfied to begin with selective partial operation with nonstriking company personnel working extended work schedules, generally twelve-hour shifts, seven days a week. Thus, an operating firm typically does not have to provide one-for-one replacement of striking workers at the outset of a strike.

The experience of the few firms that were actively involved in return-to-work movements confirms the general view that return-to-work movements have serious drawbacks. Within the sample, these companies were among the leading targets of sabotage and harassment during strikes and bitterness after strikes. Moreover, the companies had mixed results in their efforts to entice strikers back to work. A company is not legally free to take any action it chooses to induce strikers to return to work. An employer may not legally offer special inducements such as bonuses or extra benefits to striking employees to persuade them to cross the picket line.[1] Newport News Shipbuilding fared reasonably well. Another firm, however, found that only about one-quarter of its workers were willing to return to work even when confronted with the hiring of permanent replacements. A third firm fared even less well in its efforts to convince workers to return in the wake of an announced, but not yet implemented, decision to begin hiring replacements.

---

[1] *See* NLRB v. Great Dane Trailers, Inc., 388 U.S. 26 (1967).

SALARIED WORKERS

The challenge confronting a company determined to operate in the face of an effective strike is to find replacements for those workers participating in the strike. The magnitude of this challenge depends on the size of the striking bargaining unit(s) and on the scale and schedule of production planned during strike operations. Few firms attempt, at least at the outset of a strike, to maintain normal production on a normal shift basis.

The most readily available supply of potential replacement workers willing to cross a picket line to work a seven-day, twelve-hour schedule is a company's own managerial and supervisory employees. This pool of labor generally is the preferred and primary source of replacement labor among firms that operate during strikes. In most of the companies studied, this pool has provided a sufficient, if not always ample, supply of labor to meet initial operating needs.

As explained in Chapter II, managers and supervisors are not considered "employees" under the law. Therefore, they do not have the same right to engage in concerted activity that employees enjoy. Thus, generally an employer may require management and supervisory personnel to continue working during a labor dispute without regard to their membership or nonmembership in a union. Moreover, an employer is not restricted regarding the kind of work it may assign these individuals. An employer, therefore, does not commit an unfair labor practice by disciplining or discharging managerial or supervisory personnel who refuse to perform work for the employer during a labor dispute, regardless of whether the work is supervisory or nonsupervisory in nature.[2]

Nevertheless, practical problems may arise for an employer using management or supervisory employees to operate a plant during a strike if those employees are members of unions. Managers or supervisors who are members of a union may be exposed to court-collectible fines if they cross picket lines to perform rank-and-file work. A union is free to discipline supervisor-members who cross picket lines to perform work that would normally be performed by striking rank-and-file workers.[3] It may not fine supervisor-members who cross to perform purely supervisory work.[4] As for supervisory and rank-and-file work, the NLRB generally has held that a union may discipline such supervisors without violating the Act if the supervisor performs more than

---

[2] Texas Co. v. NLRB, 198 F.2d 540 (9th Cir. 1952).

[3] Florida Power & Light Co. v. IBEW Local 641, 417 U.S. 790 (1974).

[4] American Broadcasting Companies, Inc. v. Writers Guild, 437 U.S. 411 (1978).

a "minimal" amount of rank-and-file work.[5] Because the supervisors usually perform much of the required rank-and-file work during a strike, this is a likely problem.

Recruitment and Selection

The recruitment of replacement labor from among the company's existing nonbargaining-unit employees generally was structured along two dimensions: geography and occupation. Geographically, a struck location is expected to draw first upon its own resources and then upon resources from other plants in its division, other divisions, or corporate staff (typically in that order) only to the extent necessary to meet critical manpower or skill shortages. Occupationally, first-line supervisors are expected to serve as the core of the replacement work force, which is to be filled out by conscripts from the ranks of managerial (exempt) personnel and volunteers from the ranks of professional and technical personnel (exempt and nonexempt), and finally, when necessary, clerical (nonexempt) employees (invariably in that order).

The companies in the sample tended to place primary emphasis on either geography or occupation rather than a combination of the two. Most of the firms tended to view the internal supply of potential replacement labor in terms of the companywide pool of exempt supervisory and managerial personnel. A substantial minority, however, viewed that supply in terms of all exempt and nonexempt nonunion personnel at a struck facility.

First-Line Supervisors. All companies, regardless of their perceptions or priorities concerning the geographical and occupational boundaries of their in-house potential replacement force, looked to first-line supervisors as the primary source of skilled labor. These individuals routinely were assigned to strike duty or duties at their home plant and were the most widely called upon to "volunteer" for strike duty in other company plants. The rewards for the volunteer's long hours and less-than-optimal living conditions are a substantial short-term increase in earnings and a long-term increase in perceived loyalty to the company. These rewards have generally proven sufficient to ensure an adequate supply of supervisory volunteers to meet the most pressing needs of most struck facilities.

None of the companies reported a refusal of strike duty by a supervisor on grounds other than extreme personal or family hardship, and some firms recruiting supervisors for strike duty at another plant have reported greater problems in prying supervisors loose from their

---

[5] Columbia Typographical Union No. 101 (Washington Post), 242 N.L.R.B. 1079 (June 13, 1979).

bosses than from their jobs. Two of the firms in the sample, however, encountered a special problem in assigning supervisors to strike duty. In both cases, supervisory personnel were members of the striking union and were, therefore, subject to union discipline in the form of fines for crossing picket lines to perform work normally done by striking members.

Other Managerial Personnel. The second readily available source of in-house replacement labor is managerial personnel other than first-line supervisors. Most of the companies made extensive use of this pool of labor at individual plant sites. Furthermore, many of the companies reached outward from the struck plant to draw upon sales personnel attached to the plant or to the products produced in the plant, and upward to the division or company of which the plant was a part, particularly when divisional management was located on or near the site of the struck plant. Somewhat less common, although not unusual, was to find such outreach efforts extending across plants and divisions within a company. The need for technical skills most often explained cross-divisional strike duty assignments. Thus, engineering personnel were among the most likely to be drafted from other divisions or corporate staff for strike duty.

The use of managerial personnel as replacements for unionized production personnel obviously involves some potentially significant opportunity costs. No plant can operate during a strike for any length of time with only the jobs of the plant production manager and director of labor relations unaffected without some loss of organizational efficiency and control. The prospect of this loss has limited the use of managerial personnel in all companies. In most instances, managerial personnel have split their time between managerial and strike duties. The primary exception to this pattern is product and process development functions that typically are totally shut down, thus freeing all of the personnel normally assigned to those functions for full-time strike duty.

A second factor limiting utilization of managerial personnel as replacements is physical stress. The work that managers will be required to do on strike duty generally will be far more physically demanding than their work as managers, independent of the emotional stress associated with crossing a hostile picket line to work a twelve-hour shift while worrying about one's basic managerial responsibilities. Thus, it is not surprising that a number of firms reported isolated cases of health problems ranging from back problems to heart attacks among managerial personnel assigned to strike duty. All firms were sensitive to the potential for such problems and attempted to minimize them through medical screening, selective job assignment, and rotation of job assignments.

Professional, Technical, and Clerical Personnel. The third in-house source of potential replacement labor is nonunion, nonexempt professional, technical, and clerical personnel. Under the law, most clerical workers are employees and, thus, are protected if they engage in concerted activity. For example, they may not be fired for refusing to cross a picket line; they may, however, be permanently replaced for so doing.

If clerical workers are confidential employees, then they are not employees under the law, in which case they may be treated as managers or supervisors, as discussed above. The traditional standard for determining if an employee has a confidential relationship with the employer is whether the employee assists and acts in a confidential capacity to persons responsible for labor policy,[6] or has access to confidential information that may relate to collective bargaining negotiations.[7] The labor nexus standard has now been affirmed by the Supreme Court in *Hendricks County Rural Electric Membership Corp. v. NLRB.*[8]

Most firms, however, routinely expected their nonunion professional and technical personnel to be available for strike duty, and only one reported a case of refusal of strike duty by a nonunion professional or technical employee. The company hastily discharged that employee and, in so doing, committed an unfair labor practice that would not have occurred if it had replaced rather than discharged the employee in question.

The firms studied varied greatly in the extent to which they drew on clerical personnel as a source of labor to handle production operation. A few firms actively sought volunteers from their clerical staff for strike duty in the plant, generally with a fair degree of success. One company was particularly successful as a result of a rumor that the strike might force layoffs among nonunion personnel. Most companies were less aggressive in seeking volunteers for strike duty from the ranks of their clerical staff or more diffident about using volunteers to fill production as opposed to service jobs. Some firms made no attempt to utilize clerical workers as replacements. Included among these firms was at least one that employed a substantial number of spouses of production workers in clerical positions.

Several firms that have not actively recruited clerical personnel as replacements in the past indicated that they were prepared to make far

---

[6] B.F. Goodrich Co., 115 N.L.R.B. 722, 724 (1956).
[7] Pullman Standard Division, 214 N.L.R.B. 762 (1974).
[8] 50 U.S.L.W. 4037 (Dec. 1, 1981).

more extensive use of this potential source of labor in future plant operation situations. All, however, suggested that they would continue to seek volunteers only. They would not expect clerical personnel to be available for strike duty on the same basis as nonunion professional and technical employees. These companies are not yet willing to force the issue of refusal of strike duty by clerical personnel.

Assignment and Training

The assignment of jobs to replacement workers is a matter of matching job requirements and individual skills. The firms generally assign semiskilled operative and labor jobs to managerial, sales, and clerical personnel on the basis of physical capacity and any prior experience. Skilled production jobs normally are assigned to first-line supervisors. Skilled maintenance jobs are assigned to maintenance supervisors, engineering personnel, and anyone else with relevant skills or experience.

Unskilled and Semiskilled Production Jobs. Most of the companies were able to generate an ample supply of labor to fill unskilled and semiskilled production jobs from within the on-site pool of nonunion labor. Among these jobs, only those that were most demanding in terms of physical strength and stamina were difficult to fill. Such jobs often had to be rotated among a number of workers, as did some highly unpopular or unpleasant tasks, such as cleaning the cages of test animals at one pharmaceutical facility. Prior to actual operation, little or no training other than safety training generally was provided for individuals filling unskilled or semiskilled jobs. There were, however, some fairly consistent exceptions to this rule, most notably in the case of forklift operators.

Skilled Production Jobs. Skilled production jobs proved more difficult to fill. In about one-half of all operating experiences, firms were able to develop a sufficient supply of labor to fill these positions using supervisory, engineering, and technical personnel from within the struck facility. In the balance of the cases, companies were unable to meet their needs in this area using local sources and had to import supervisory personnel from other plants. Included among these cases was one company that was able to operate one of two struck plants only by pooling the supervisory manpower of both plants.

In most cases, supervisory personnel needed little or no training to assume jobs performed by workers under their supervision. When retraining was deemed advisable, it generally took the form of observing or working alongside the individual whose job was to be filled in the event of a strike. Individuals less familiar with the specific operations and equipment that they would confront on the job were given more extensive training, often utilizing a combination of formal classroom training using materials developed for hourly employees and the same type of on-the-job training utilized for supervisory personnel.

Surprisingly, the use of on-the-job training prior to a possible strike has not encountered strong, overt resistance from unions or workers in most plants, although it often is a subject of conversation in negotiations. Only one firm indicated that it had encountered sufficient resistance to induce it to abandon the practice. No other firm reported being similarly pressed, and most indicated a strong commitment to prestrike on-the-job training, if only because of the signal it sends to both the union and the workers of the company's willingness and ability to operate during a strike.

Maintenance Work. The most difficult replacement problem for virtually all of the companies studied was maintenance. Most firms could not find or train a sufficient number of skilled replacement workers in-house at a struck plant to fill their basic maintenance needs. Thus, maintenance personnel typically were imported from other company locations on a fairly extensive basis. Absent the import option, a company can only "pray for no major breakdowns and patch those which do occur." This was the situation in two of the plants studied in their initial experience, but it is unusual among more experienced firms, which generally take great pains to avoid this problem.

Most companies were able to meet basic maintenance needs during strike operations with a combination of local and imported personnel. Indeed, in a few situations, prestrike maintenance backlogs actually were reduced during the course of strike operations as a result of a combination of greater efficiency in the form of operator performance of routine maintenance jobs and good fortune in the form of few serious breakdowns. In the vast majority of operating situations, however, firms were able only to hold their own even when major scheduled maintenance jobs had been completed before the strike. All firms, even the most fortunate, readily admitted that "maintenance is always a headache."

Terms and Conditions

The acceptance of strike duty involves a commitment for a period of time. For those supervisory personnel normally employed in the struck plant, that commitment is "for the duration." For other employees not normally employed in production or engineering operations in the struck plant, that commitment generally is for a limited period of time. A few firms assigned personnel or accepted volunteers on the basis of a two-week commitment. Most firms, however, have found that two-week stints of strike duty are too short to permit employees to be highly productive replacement workers and, therefore, assign personnel on the basis of four-week commitments. Those firms apparently also have found that four weeks is too long to ask workers to go without seeing their families. Thus, those firms endeavored to provide every employee with every other weekend off and reimbursed imported employees for a trip home on their weekend off.

Work Schedule. In the early stages of plant operation, the basic work schedule for individuals on strike duty in most of the firms studied was twelve-hour shifts, seven days a week. Only two firms had a sufficient supply of in-house replacement labor to operate on a normal basis (eight-hour shifts, five days a week). One other company was able to meet its goals by using a nearly normal schedule (twelve-hour shifts, five days a week).

An eighty-four-hour workweek is not impractical at the outset of operation, when emotions generally are high, but is not viable for an extended period of time. This was clearly recognized by the companies studied, all of which were committed to moving toward normal work schedules as quickly as the supply of replacement labor would permit. The first step in this process typically was an effort to shorten the workweek by providing all personnel with at least two days of every two weeks off rather than by reducing the shift length. Two companies chose to shorten the workday rather than the workweek, but both were operating almost exclusively with local personnel in the face of little or no union effort to inhibit access to the plant. Only a very few firms were able to go substantially beyond such initial efforts to "normalize" work schedules, and most of those were able to do so only because they were willing either to accept very limited operation or to recruit outside replacement labor.

Rate of Pay. Individuals on strike duty were paid at their normal rate of pay or the rate for the job performed on strike duty—whichever was higher. As required by federal wage-hour laws, premium pay at the rate of time and one-half was paid for all overtime hours spent on strike duty. In addition, one company voluntarily provided an "inconvenience premium" for work on holidays and on a seventh consecutive day. In most cases, individuals on strike duty continued to receive their normal salary check plus a separate check for overtime hours worked in the plant on strike duty.

The work schedules of most firms during strike operation afforded individuals on strike duty ample opportunity to earn extra income. Extra income is a definite incentive for employees to volunteer for strike duty when they have that choice. It also encourages individuals to expand the number of overtime hours worked or reported as worked. Thus, most companies have developed procedures for keeping track of hours worked on strike duty and policies governing how time spent in the plant is to be treated in calculating overtime hours worked.

A number of firms indicated concern about inequities in the extra earnings opportunities afforded by strike duty. Specifically, they pointed to the fact that the first-line supervisors who worked the most skilled production jobs typically had salary rates and, therefore, overtime earnings less than the employees filling less skilled jobs and working under their supervision. This inequity often was compounded by the fact that supervisors frequently did not get days off as did their lower-skilled, higher-paid subordinates because their skills could not be spared. At least three firms felt compelled to address this problem by awarding a poststrike bonus to supervisory and other nonmanagerial personnel who served strike duty. Those bonuses ranged from a $100 bill to five extra vacation days.

Provisions for In-House Replacements. Most firms routinely plan to house and feed their in-house replacement employees during the initial days of plant operation until ingress and egress to the plant can be reasonably assured. Once entry and exit of the plant has been accomplished, it is no longer necessary to house replacement personnel in-plant, although it continues to be necessary to provide accommodations for imported personnel. As long as twelve-hour shifts continue to be used, however, firms have found it advantageous, if not strictly necessary, to continue to provide in-plant meal service.

All of the firms made extensive and expensive efforts to provide ample high quality meals in-plant, particularly when replacements were required to live on-site. The extent of the effort can be judged from the experience of one company that spent $1.1 million over three months to provide a daily average of 1,000 breakfasts, 2,500 lunches, and 800 dinners. That company and others that made similar efforts agreed that good meals were a crucial factor in building and sustaining morale, although several also admitted that it was possible to overdo a good thing in terms of caloric intakes. Most firms did not take the same positive view regarding the serving of beer or other alcoholic beverages at end-of-shift happy hours. Many firms that tried happy hours found it advisable to abandon them.

The use of imported personnel obviously requires that arrangements be made for transportation and accommodation of these employees while on strike duty. Most firms arranged and paid directly for travel, hotel accommodations, and rental cars for imported employees and compensated them for other living expenses on an actual cost basis. Few firms reported serious problems in this area. One firm reported that it had inadvertently cornered the local market in rental cars, a problem it solved and others have avoided by mandatory car pooling of imported employees. A second company encountered a different problem when it housed a number of imported employees in a motel, the bar of which was frequented regularly by bargaining-unit members, a problem that it resolved and that others have avoided by more judicious selection of accommodations for imported personnel.

Productivity and Morale

The companies studied were unanimous in asserting that they were able to keep the productivity and morale of in-house replacements high throughout the course of strike operations. There were start-up productivity problems, but once those problems were overcome, the quantity and quality of product turned out by replacements typically were reported to have been at least equal to normal standards. Similarly, several companies noted an apparent decline in the morale of replacements as the novelty of strike duty wore off, but also reported that replacements did not take long to get their "second wind."

The fact that replacement workers equalled or exceeded normal productivity standards was attributed to both their ingenuity in performing the tasks assigned them and their lack of adherence to traditional definitions of job content and limits. These adventures beyond normal work practice and jurisdiction, all asserted, created no new safety or health problems. Not one firm reported an abnormally high incidence of accidents or injuries during strike operations. Most firms, however, did acknowledge a high incidence of blisters, sore muscles, and similarly minor physical problems among replacements, particularly in the early stages of strike operation.

The key to the sustained morale of replacements was attributed by most firms to the spontaneous development of a "will to win" and "sense of common cause." These psychological forces, most admitted, were important factors in virtually eliminating the problem of turnover among in-house replacements. Although turnover was not a problem for any of the firms, several admitted that the strain of crossing a picket line to work long hours at physical labor took its toll, particularly on sales and staff personnel, who often were obviously relieved when their stint of strike duty was over.

High productivity and morale may be spontaneous phenomena in the early stages of operation, but they are not self-sustaining. Virtually all of the firms indicated that they made conscious and consistent efforts to keep both morale and productivity high. The key to success in such efforts in the view of all of the firms asked was effective communication to inform replacements of what is going on in the plant (e.g., production levels, progress in negotiations) coupled with statements and other demonstrations of appreciation and support from management at all levels. Communication and appreciation, however, are not without their limits. They must be supported by a comprehensive personnel relations effort to deal with the problems of a "new work force"—a work force that, as at least one company admitted, probably would soon begin to think like the work force it had replaced if its problems were left unattended.

REPLACEMENT WORKERS

A third option open to the employer attempting to man a struck plant is to hire outside personnel as a supplement to or substitute for company personnel in replacing striking bargaining-unit members. Basically, the exercise of this option involves a decision to hire replacements on either a temporary or permanent basis in the local labor market. Such hiring may be done directly or indirectly through the use of contractors.

An employer has a legal right to hire replacements for striking workers subject to legal constraints on the use of "professional strikebreakers." An employer also may legally subcontract bargaining-unit work on a temporary basis during a strike in order to continue serving its customers.

The Decision to Hire Replacements

The hiring of replacements for bargaining-unit employees or the subcontracting of bargaining-unit work was not an integral element in the operating plans of most of the firms studied. Only three of the companies indicated that their basic operating plans were predicated on the hiring of outside personnel to perform bargaining-unit work. Only one of these three companies indicated that this approach was a matter of policy rather than necessity. Specifically, it was the policy of that firm to inform its unions that it would hire outside replacements in the event that a strike appeared likely to last long enough to threaten the adequacy of the inventories built in anticipation of it. Until that point was reached, it was the policy of the company not to attempt to operate struck facilities.

Although the hiring of outside replacements and use of outside contractors is not an integral element in most operating plans, those options have been used by many of the firms studied, albeit sparingly and reluctantly, as a last resort. When these options have been used, they generally have been adopted on an ad hoc basis in response to problems encountered in operating with company personnel. It was the companies with more labor-intensive production processes that most frequently took this course of action.

The apparent reluctance of most firms to resort to the use of outside replacements reflected, in part, a desire to avoid further antagonizing unions and workers. This consideration, however, often appeared less important than the perceived low probability of success in securing outside replacement labor. Thus, even in dire straits, a number of firms chose not to seek replacement labor. In short, a company deciding whether to replace, like a company deciding whether to operate, may be constrained as much by the fear of failure as by the fear of confrontation.

The institutional consequences associated with the fear of confrontation did play an important role in determining the type of replacement labor hired. About one-quarter of the firms had not used any type of replacement labor in their most recent or salient cases of plant operation. Another one-quarter of the companies reported using "supplementary" rather than "replacement" labor to augment company personnel in their most recent or salient cases of plant operation. The use of supplementary labor included: (1) deferring the retirement of salaried personnel and recalling salaried personnel recently retired; (2) expanding use of existing on-site contractor personnel; (3) hiring temporary supervisory or security personnel; and (4) hiring new workers in anticipation of attrition during the strike. The remaining one-half of the companies reported some recent effort to replace striking workers either directly or indirectly. Most of those firms, however, consciously avoided the use of permanent replacements either by explicitly stating that they were hiring only temporary replacements or by being silent on the subject of whether replacements were temporary or permanent.

The Hiring of Replacements

The same fear of failure that tempered the use of outside replacements also influenced the recruitment of replacements once the decision to hire was made. All of the companies that sought replacements on the open market reported extensive efforts to ensure the success of that quest. Thus, none of the companies were satisfied simply to run carefully worded want ads in the hope of attracting the needed applicants. Most actively sought to test the market and to develop informal recruiting channels before "going public." One firm, as a matter of policy, made sure it had at least forty to fifty individuals lined up to apply for employment before it ran any ads. Most firms were prepared to conduct interviews with applicants off-site in order to avoid forcing applicants to confront a picket line in search of a job.

All of the firms that sought outside replacement labor reported surprising success in that search in terms of the number of applications received and the number of applicants willing to cross a picket line to file applications, even when that was unnecessary. Indeed, one firm was so inundated with applications that it used willingness to cross the picket line to file an application as an initial screening device. The reported success of the companies studied may reflect their skill in deciding where and when to seek replacements, or simply the selective memory of company officials. In any event, it has not yet greatly enhanced their enthusiasm for using replacement workers as a basic part of their plant operation strategy.

The Experience with Replacements

Although most firms reported no serious problems in the effective use of replacement labor, one firm that did experience problems was willing to admit and discuss such problems openly. That company initially hired temporary replacements but was forced to hire permanent replacements. Its experience with temporary replacements was extremely favorable, primarily because it was able to draw heavily on college students seeking summer employment who were not fussy about what they did and who were anxious to avail themselves of the earnings opportunities provided by twelve-hour shifts. The company's experience with permanent replacements hired after the end of the summer, however, was far less satisfactory. The firm experienced high turnover among permanent replacements, which the company attributed to the fact that many had not done physical labor before and had been forced into such work by a lack of alternative employment opportunities. Thus, many left as soon as alternatives became available, resulting in both high training costs and low productivity for the company.

This same firm also discussed at length the problems it encountered in integrating its replacements with the striking forces once a settlement was reached, problems that were common to all firms that hired other than strictly temporary replacements. The first such problem arises out of the striking union's demand for immediate recall of all striking workers. Returning strikers, although entitled to preferential hiring upon the departure of such replacements, have no legal right to displace employees hired as permanent replacements. Companies that hire permanent replacements are typically unwilling to grant job rights to returning strikers beyond those afforded by the law and have, therefore, rejected union demands for immediate reinstatement of all strikers. Two firms, however, were able both to reject and to accommodate this demand. They consciously had hired only enough permanent replacements to fill the number of job openings that they anticipated would be created by attrition by the end of the strike.

The company in question also reported the expected poststrike bitterness within its work force between those who stayed out for the duration of the strike and those who reported to work. The latter group included the "scabs"—those who returned to work when the company began to hire permanent replacements—and the "superscabs"—permanent replacements. Similar internal divisions were reported by other firms, although the distinction between "scabs" and "superscabs" often was reversed. In either event, turnover among these disdained classes of workers tended to be high in the months following the end of the strike.

Most of the firms that have exercised the option to hire permanent replacements have not experienced these integration problems on a significant scale because of the union's responses to the threat of hiring permanent replacements, backed by the placing of ads and the taking of applications. The union may respond by hardening its position and pursuing its demands indefinitely, as was the case in a few instances in which companies reported ongoing multiyear strikes in specific plants operating with permanent replacements. Alternatively, and more typically, the union may decide to soften its position and seek a quick settlement, as was the case in a clear majority of the cases. In either event, work force integration is not likely to be a significant problem.

SUBCONTRACTING

During a strike a company may legally subcontract bargaining-unit work on a temporary basis in order to continue serving its customers.[9] The law is not definite, but an employer probably also may permanently subcontract work during a strike after notifying the union and bargaining to an impasse.[10]

Even if a company is legally able to subcontract work from a struck plant, however, such action may not successfully circumvent a labor dispute. Depending on the nature of the work subcontracted, striking employees may lawfully picket a subcontractor. The issue revolves

---

[9] Empire Terminal Warehouse Company, 151 N.L.R.B. 1359 (1965), *aff'd*, 355 F.2d 842 (D.C. Cir. 1966). *See also* Shell Oil Company, 149 N.L.R.B. 283 (1964).

[10] American Cyanamid Co. v. NLRB, 592 F.2d 356 (7th Cir. 1979). The court here based its decision that an employer could permanently subcontract work during a strike after bargaining to an impasse on the holding of Fibreboard Paper Products Corp. v. NLRB, 379 U.S. 203 (1964). In *Fibreboard* the Supreme Court said that subcontracting is

around whether a company that accepts such work remains a neutral employer under the National Labor Relations Act, and thus is protected against secondary boycotts.[11]

If the subcontractor does work that, but for the strike, would have been performed by the employees of the struck employer, then the subcontractor legally may be an ally of the struck company, and therefore may be lawfully picketed.[12] Two additional elements must be demonstrated to establish an ally relationship.

First, the effect of having the struck work performed by others must enable a struck employer to avoid the economic pressures of a strike. A company is found to avoid the economic pressures of a strike through subcontracting whenever it is able to keep customers, i.e., not lose business, because the subcontractor has met the given customers' needs during the strike.[13] This test is not particularly difficult to satisfy, as generally at least some business is saved, or not lost, because of the efforts of a given subcontractor or subcontractors during a strike.

Second, the subcontractor must have performed the work pursuant to an arrangement with the company on strike. Thus, if, on their own initiative, customers of the struck employer go to another company and ask it to do their work, this second company is not an ally of the struck employer.[14] Clearly, however, a direct contractual agreement between the company on strike and the given subcontractor is unnecessary in order to find an arrangement subjecting the subcontractor to allied status. Such an arrangement may be inferred by the NLRB and the courts upon examination of all the facts and circumstances involved.[15]

Because of the potential secondary picketing problems, subcontracting of work during a strike in order to circumvent the labor dispute can only succeed after careful long-term planning. Realistically, even after careful planning, subcontracting is not a viable means for most companies to supply their customers' needs. It is, therefore, not a practical alternative to operation. Subcontracting, however, may serve to satisfy specific needs that are difficult to satisfy using replacement labor.

---

a mandatory subject of bargaining; thus, an employer may only unilaterally act after bargaining to a bona fide impasse. *Contra,* Hawaii Meat Company, Ltd. v. NLRB, 321 F.2d 397 (9th Cir. 1963).

[11] NLRA § 8(b)(4), 29 U.S.C. § 158(b)(4).

[12] *See* Douds v. Metropolitan Fed'n of Architects, Engineers, Chemists and Technicians, Local 231, 75 F. Supp. 672 (S.D.N.Y. 1948).

[13] *See, e.g.,* GAIU, Local No. 277 (S & M Rotogravure Service, Inc.), 219 N.L.R.B. 1053 (1975), *review denied,* 540 F.2d 1304 (7th Cir. 1976).

[14] *See* Blackhawk Engraving Co. v. NLRB, 540 F.2d 1296, 1302 (7th Cir. 1976).

[15] *See, e.g.,* Mount Morris GAIU, Local No. 91-P (Blackhawk Engraving Co.), 219 N.L.R.B. 1030 (1975), *enforced,* 540 F.2d 1296 (7th Cir. 1976).

SUMMARY

The most fundamental challenge confronting an employer that intends to operate a struck facility is to recruit an adequate supply of labor to perform the bargaining-unit work in that facility. There are three potential sources for that supply: (1) members of the bargaining unit who are disenchanted with the strike action; (2) managerial, supervisory, and other nonunion company personnel; and (3) individuals willing to enter the employ of the company as temporary or permanent replacements.

Historically, return-to-work movements have been viewed as an essential underpinning of the ability of employers to operate during strikes. For the most part, that is no longer the case. Employers generally do not plan to rely on disenchanted bargaining-unit personnel. They neither encourage nor welcome return-to-work movements as part of their basic plant operation strategy. Thus, except in truly unusual cases, plant operation no longer entails the explosiveness of back-to-work movements.

Managerial and supervisory personnel are the primary source of replacement labor. With the exception of relatively labor-intensive operations or prolonged strikes, this in-house source of clearly temporary replacement labor generally has proven adequate, if not ample, to meet the firms' operating needs. Thus, as a rule, plant operation does not directly challenge "the union's status as exclusive bargaining agent for workers in the unit nor the status of those workers as employees of the company."

Employers have not widely relied upon either new hiring or subcontracting as a source of labor to man struck facilities. This limited use of outside replacements reflects the same fear of failure and fear of confrontation that deters firms from attempting to operate in the first place. Despite those fears, some operating firms have been forced, more out of desperation than animosity toward the union, to seek outside replacement labor. As in the case of plant operation itself, they typically have found their fears to have been unjustified. Nevertheless, few firms base their operating plans on the use of outside replacements. Most continue to view the hiring of outside replacements, particularly permanent replacements, as an option to be exercised only in unusual cases, and even then more with a view toward breaking an impasse than breaking a strike. Success in replacing workers will give employers added courage in exercising this option for offensive as well as defensive reasons.

CHAPTER V

The Logistics of Operation: Access

After the recruitment of sufficient manpower, the next major challenge facing an employer that attempts to operate during a strike is to maintain access of vital personnel, goods, and services to the struck facility. The two basic weapons employed by unions to limit that access are picketing and boycotts.

THE MOVEMENT OF PERSONNEL

Any company that finds itself party to a strike must expect that the union will picket its facility to inform the public of the existence of a labor dispute and to dissuade nonstriking employees from reporting for work. Any attempt to operate must be expected to and will intensify those union efforts. Typically, intensified efforts at dissuasion range from mass picketing to harassment of those nonstriking employees who attempt to report to work. Most of the firms studied reported that mass picketing was routine in cases of plant operation. Other commonplace picket line incidents included the hurling of epithets, the scattering of nails, the slashing of tires, and the scratching of cars as nonstriking workers endeavored to enter a struck plant. At one plant acts such as these resulted in $50,000 in uninsured damages to employees' vehicles. Vehicle damage at a second plant included:

1. flat tires   2,000
2. tires ruined   32
3. windshields broken   28
4. paint on cars   26
5. antennas broken   22
6. pounds of nails picked up   245

Picket line harassment forces nonstriking employees to run a formidable gauntlet in electing to report to work. Their willingness and ability to confront that challenge is one factor that must be considered in the development of an operating plan. In that context, firms typically tend to identify three groups of employees—nonstriking unionized

employees, nonunion clerical personnel, and managerial and supervisory personnel.

Nonstriking Unionized Personnel

Those employers with multiple bargaining units in a single plant
must consider the effects of a strike by members of one bargaining unit
on the willingness of members of other units to report to work. Among
the companies studied, the experience in this area varied widely, but
more often than not was unfavorable, at least at the outset of a strike.
Thus, most firms planned to operate on the assumption that no unionized company personnel would cross a picket line.

Several companies reported specific instances in which the picket
line of a fairly small unit did not deter members of a much larger unit
from reporting to work. The members of the larger unit, however,
typically refused to perform work normally done by members of the
strike unit, even, as in one case, when the alternative to performing
that work was layoff. A substantial number of companies reported instances in which members of a small bargaining unit refused to cross
the picket line of a larger unit. The single most prevalent, and often
most troublesome, such case was the refusal of power plant operators
and truck drivers to cross the picket line of production workers.

An employer is not defenseless in the face of such a sympathy strike.
Legally, an employer may not discharge employees simply because
they engage in such activity. It may, however, permanently replace
employees who decline to cross the picket line of another bargaining
unit, as one firm did in the case of a small but critical unit of power
plant operators, albeit with considerable difficulty. Moreover, an employer may seek to compel sympathy strikers and their union to honor
their collective bargaining agreement and return to work, but this may
be a time-consuming and uncertain course of action, possibly involving
recourse to both arbitration and the courts.

Sympathy strikers are afforded the same protection under the law
as economic strikers.[1] Similarly, sympathy strikers face the same
liabilities; they plight their troth with the strikers, and thus may be
permanently replaced.[2]

If the right to engage in a sympathy strike has been raised in a collective bargaining agreement, as it may be,[3] then an employer may
either discharge the sympathy strikers for engaging in illegal activity[4]

---

[1] Redwing Carriers, Inc., 137 N.L.R.B. 1545, *enforced*, 325 F.2d 1011 (D.C. Cir. 1963),
cert. denied, 377 U.S. 905 (1964).

[2] NLRB v. Southern Greyhound Lines, 426 F.2d 1299, 1301 (5th Cir. 1970).

[3] NLRB v. Rockaway News Supply Co., 345 U.S. 71 (1953).

[4] NLRB v. Sands Mfg. Co., 306 U.S. 332 (1939).

or may attempt to compel those employees to fulfill their contractual obligations. Injunctive relief from a sympathy strike that violates a contractual no-strike clause was discussed in Chapter II. Injunctive relief is not automatic:[5] an employer must first seek arbitration of the issue. The arbitral decision may, in turn, be enforced, and injunctive relief secured.

The problem of sympathy strikes has not yet extended beyond other bargaining units in the struck plant. None of the companies reported instances in which unionized employees in a nonstruck plant refused to work in support of their union brethren in a struck plant the company was operating. This was true even when members of the bargaining unit in the nonstruck plant were temporarily assigned to supervisory positions to fill in for supervisory personnel sent to help operate the struck plant. This apparent lack of "common cause" may reflect simply what most companies noted: a lack of effort on the part of the striking unions to enlist the sympathy of workers and unions in nonstruck plants. A few firms, however, noted a lack of sympathy even among those workers and unions asked by the striking union to cooperate in its job action.

Nonunion Clerical Personnel

The basic planning assumption of most firms was that nonunion clerical personnel would be willing to cross the picket line to report for work on their normal jobs. Thus, most firms explicitly communicated to such personnel the company's expectation that they would report for work on a business-as-usual basis despite a strike. Nevertheless, under the law, most clerical workers are employees and, thus, are protected if they engage in concerted activity. For example, they may not be fired for refusing to cross a picket line; they may, however, be permanently replaced for so doing. In all cases, the expectation that clerical personnel would report for work was supported by efforts to condition workers to the problems that they might face in crossing the picket line and inform them of the way in which such problems should be handled.

While most firms expected their clerical personnel to report for work during a strike, a substantial number felt that they could not rely on the willingness and ability of clerical personnel to "run the gauntlet" of a picket line as the basis for maintaining essential clerical operations. Thus, a number of firms made arrangements to relocate key clerical operations to off-site work locations in preparation for a possible

---

[5] Buffalo Forge Co. v. United Steelworkers of America, 428 U.S. 397 (1976).

strike, and several others arranged to "convoy" in such personnel, if necessary, by train or bus during the early stages of a strike. Furthermore, most companies pursued relatively lenient policies in excusing clerical personnel who claimed to have been deterred from reporting to work by real or threatened potentially violent confrontations while attempting to cross a picket line. Specifically, most firms assumed that nonunion clerical workers who failed to cross the picket line did so out of fear rather than sympathy and, therefore, took no action to replace them.

The basic expectation of firms that their nonunion clerical personnel would report for work typically was fulfilled. Although these workers often were subjected to the same harassment as other personnel in crossing the picket line, they typically were not the subject of the same antipathy as were managerial and supervisory personnel. In addition, most clerical employees exhibited a surprising degree of resolve to report to work—despite the lack of strong sanctions for not doing so—which carried most of them through all but the most massive and violent of picket line activities. Thus, virtually all of the firms reported being able to maintain basic clerical activities with relatively little difficulty throughout the course of plant operation, although not without some sporadic problems when picket line activity became particularly intense.

Managerial and Supervisory Personnel

Managerial and supervisory personnel routinely are expected to be willing to cross a picket line to report for strike duty and are subject to discharge for failure to do so. None of the firms studied indicated any lack of confidence in their managerial and supervisory employees in this respect. A few reported that overenthusiasm rather than reluctance was a problem. Although none of the firms doubted the *willingness* of their managerial and supervisory personnel to cross a picket line, they were divided with respect to their perceptions of the likelihood that such personnel would, in fact, be *able* to cross it.

A firm that is unwilling to run the risk of testing the ability of its key managerial and supervisory "replacement" workers to cross a picket line must be prepared to operate a struck plant under a state of siege. The prospect of a siege requires that management choose between two strategic options in preparing to operate: (1) it may attempt to break the siege relying on its own ingenuity and that of its employees, with the benefit of whatever assistance it can secure from local and state police in moving personnel into and out of the plant; or (2) it may accept the siege and prepare to operate without moving personnel into and out of the plant, at least until it can force a lifting of the siege by court order.

Most of the companies studied prepared to operate on the assumption that only the second of these two options could be counted on. These firms routinely were prepared to bring key replacement personnel into the plant prior to the strike deadline and to house and feed those personnel in-plant for an extended period of time, if necessary.

The fact that most firms studied were prepared to operate under a state of siege did not mean, however, that all were equally resigned to or sanguine about that prospect. A majority of these firms made no serious attempt to establish ingress or egress for replacement personnel until after an injunction limiting picket activity was secured. These companies had to pay a price in terms of the in-plant housing and feeding expense of replacement personnel.

A minority of the firms, however, rejected this passive strategy to pursue a policy of aggressively attempting to force the picket line on their own. These companies had to pay a price in the form of harassment and violence on the picket line. Those that elected to pay this price generally are convinced that it was not an excessive one in terms of what was gained in psychological or strategic advantage by demonstrating the resolve and ability of the company to operate. A few of the firms that have not elected to pay this price apparently have come to the same conclusion and are now ready to consider the option of forcing picket lines in future plant operation situations. Most firms, however, continue to be committed to a more conservative and passive approach.

THE PROVISION OF GOODS AND SERVICES

The movement of company personnel into and out of a struck plant in the face of picketing activity is only one of the problems confronting an employer that attempts to operate. A second, equally important problem created by a strike and picketing is that of maintaining access to necessary goods and services normally provided by other employers. Specifically, any employer that decides to operate must anticipate the possibility that picketing will deter employees of other employers from entering a struck facility to deliver goods or provide services.

The most obvious and troublesome interruption in service is the refusal of unionized transport personnel to cross a picket line to deliver raw materials or pick up finished goods. There are, however, other possibilities. Employees of contractors performing on-site construction or maintenance work or providing janitorial or food service may refuse to cross a picket line, and suppliers and customers may be reluctant to do business with a struck facility.

Shipping and Receiving

Picketing activity may inhibit the flow of goods into and out of a struck plant even if it does not physically block access to it. Transport workers, who are generally unionized, frequently honor picket lines as a matter of principle rather than under duress. Unions that are aware of this fact often actively seek to gain the support of transport workers independent of resource to a picket line. The success of such efforts in the case of the companies studied was less than complete. Nonetheless, all companies felt compelled to plan for operation on the basis that unionized transport personnel would refuse to cross a picket line.

The prospect of a curtailment of transport service induced most firms to build inventories of supplies and raw materials as well as to reduce stocks of finished goods in-plant prior to contract expiration. At best, such action was a stopgap measure designed to permit the plant to continue operation during the early stages of a strike when access to the plant was likely to be physically blocked. A few firms whose raw materials and finished products were shipped by pipeline were able to operate for a prolonged period without access to other means of transport, but most lacked the physical capacity to store sufficient raw materials or finished products to sustain operations for more than a fairly short period of time. Thus, with few exceptions, the firms studied carefully planned and prepared to maintain their capacity to receive and ship goods in the face of a picket line.

Transport Options and Strategies. The transport options open to management under strike conditions include: (1) relying on supervisory employees of contract carriers; (2) hiring nonunion contract carriers; and (3) training and licensing nonunion company personnel to perform carrier work. The first option has been the one most widely used by the companies studied, most of which reported good cooperation and reasonable success, particularly in the case of rail transportation. The second option is not possible in the case of rail transport and often is not feasible in the case of maritime transport. In the case of truck transport, however, a number of firms have reported good results in relying on nonunion trucking firms that specialize in serving struck plants. The third option has been used to a limited extent by several companies to supplement nonunion carrier personnel in providing truck transport, but only two companies rely on this option as an integral element of their truck transport operating plan. Both of those firms are strongly committed to plant operation and have decided that an in-house supply of qualified, licensed, nonunion truck drivers is necessary to ensure the credibility of that commitment.

The strategies of the firms studied with respect to the movement of goods across the picket line, particularly by truck, paralleled their strategies with respect to the movement of personnel. A majority of firms would not openly challenge a picket line by attempting to move trucks into or out of the plant unless it was absolutely necessary. These firms typically attempted to meet their truck transport needs by other means—helicopter, barge, or train—or by sneaking trucks into and out of the plant through remote gates or on midnight runs. A minority of the firms, however, pursued more aggressive strategies, such as the use of convoys and surprise daylight runs. As in the case of the movement of personnel, these firms paid a price for their aggressiveness in terms of trouble on the picket line—a price perceived to be justified by the strategic advantage gained by a show of determination to maintain all avenues of access to a struck plant.

For the most part, the transport problems created by picketing have not extended beyond the plant site. A number of companies routinely establish remote warehouse sites to receive and ship goods. All attempts to keep the location of these sites secret have been reasonably successful. As a result, none of the firms reported any picket activity at such sites. Picketing of marine and truck terminals also was not a common occurrence or major problem, although a few cases of such activity were reported. A few companies, however, were sufficiently concerned about this possibility to alter their normal shipping routes. In at least one case, this precautionary measure cost the plant a considerable amount of money in added transport costs. Most companies did not think it necessary to take similar precautions to avoid off-site problems in the handling of company cargo by neutral employers.

Contract and Public Services

The possibility that a strike and picketing will curtail access to services provided on-site by contractor personnel cannot be discounted by an employer that plans to operate during a strike. The work most often done by contractor personnel is construction that normally is not essential to plant operation. Contractors also, however, perform maintenance and janitorial work that in many plants is essential in maintaining plant operation. Finally, a number of firms are dependent on outside contractors for meal service, which may become crucial in the event of plant operation.

Construction and Maintenance Work. Continuity of contractor services for construction and maintenance work not normally done by bargaining-unit members was not a major problem for most of the firms studied. An employer may set up a reserved gate, immune from picketing, through which a contractor's employees can enter, providing that (1) the work of the contractor is not related to the normal operation of the plant, and (2) the work, if done when the plant is operating regularly, would not necessitate a curtailing of the plant's operation.[6] If noncontractor employees use the gate, however, the union is free to picket all entrances to the premises.

Reserved gates for the employees of such contractors were common and highly, if not totally, effective in obviating the necessity for these employees to cross a picket line to perform their work. Many of the firms reported some picket activity at reserved gates, resulting in varying degrees of service curtailment. But in all cases this problem had been anticipated and was quickly solved by the threat or filing of unfair labor practice charges. In several cases, unions raised questions regarding the use of contractor personnel to perform bargaining-unit work. Most firms were able to respond by inviting union officials to tour the plant and check the work being done by contractor personnel. These tours normally not only answered the union's allegations but also permitted the company an opportunity to prove that it was operating the plant successfully.

Janitorial and Food Services.   Several firms reported problems with contractors providing janitorial or food service. Some firms did not have separate gates for such contractor personnel prior to a strike and were not totally successful in establishing such gates after the strike began, in part because the strike itself forced expanded use of contractor services. Most firms avoided these problems by relying on nonunion contractors, some of whom specialize in providing service to struck plants. Other firms had to make do by using clerical personnel for food service and housecleaning duties. One firm encountered problems with local health authorities because it was relying on such personnel to prepare food at home as well as to serve it in the plant. That same company encountered another food problem when the merchandise in its vending machines went bad because its contractor's employees would not cross the picket line to service the machines. Finally, a few companies experienced problems with refuse removal, which forced some of them to resort to smuggling trash out in the trunks of nonstriking employees' cars.

Public or Utility Services.   The possibility that a picket line will limit access to essential public or utility services also concerned several firms. For the most part, those concerns proved to be unfounded, as none of the companies studied reported any unusual problems of lack of cooperation in their dealings with public utilities or other providers

---

[6] *See* Local 761, International Union of Electrical Workers v. NLRB (General Electric Co.), 366 U.S. 667 (1961).

of local services. One company did report some delay in getting the local power company to repair a transformer located on the plant site, but most firms praised the cooperation of both private utilities and public services in the event of a breakdown or emergency.

Community Interest in the Strike

The minimal problems encountered by the companies studied in maintaining access to public services were, in most cases, accompanied by a similar lack of problems in dealing with local elected officials. Most of the firms studied reported relatively little community interest in their decision to operate during a strike. The few firms that did report such interest indicated that it was more their "intransigence" at the bargaining table than their decision to operate that was the focus of attention. Only one firm reported that its decision to operate a plant had become a political issue in the local community. Only two others reported instances in which the union actively sought to make the decision to operate a political issue—without notable success. Thus, it is not surprising that only a few of the firms studied are sufficiently apprehensive about the local political consequences of a decision to operate to undertake an aggressive public relations campaign to defend that decision, although most firms were prepared to do so if necessary. In most cases, that need has not arisen and firms have been better served by a policy of avoiding public discussion and debate over their decision to operate.

Supplier and Customer Boycotts

The goal of an employer that elects to operate during a strike is to be able to continue to do business as usual. Those with whom it does business, however, may not feel free to continue their normal business relations with the struck employer out of concern over the potential consequences of "aiding and abetting" that employer in its efforts to operate. The possibility of a "boycott" action by suppliers or customers, an avenue open to unions in their efforts to deter or impede operation, is thus one other factor to consider in the decision to operate.

As a general proposition, a union may not legally pressure either suppliers or customers to stop dealing with a struck company. In certain recent situations unions have attempted to organize boycotts of companies against which the unions have disputes. The law affords a company substantial protection against such threats:[7] the NLRA specifically

---

[7] National Labor Relations Act, § 8(b)(4), 49 Stat. 449 (1935), 29 U.S.C. § 158(b)(4).

provides for injunctive relief against secondary boycotts.[8] This protection is generally adequate to ensure the availability of supplies and customers for the finished goods. The law, however, allows a union to publicize a labor dispute and to urge a consumer boycott of neutral employers that carry products of the struck employer.

The law is designated to protect neutral businesses not directly involved in a given labor dispute from economic pressures by a striking union. Thus, secondary boycott analysis requires determining which business or businesses are primary participants in a labor dispute with the given union and which businesses are involved only in a secondary or indirect way.

The law in this area may be particularly important to a multiplant, multidivision company because the nonstriking businesses of the same owner may legally be subject to union picketing if those businesses are determined to be the primary employer.[9]

Single Employer Test. The critical distinction in determining who may be legally subject to union picketing is whether a "single employer" relationship exists. On the one hand, separately incorporated entities may, for labor law purposes, be deemed a single employer. On the other hand, divisions of a parent corporation that are not separately incorporated may be deemed to be separate employers. If separate business entities are found to be a single employer, all are the primary employer when a union strikes one of their number; thus, a union may lawfully picket any of the entities. In contrast, when various business entities are determined to be separate employers, a union dispute with one of them will not afford the union the right to lawfully picket the other; union picketing of the separate or secondary employers violates the law.

The United States Supreme Court has specifically endorsed a four-pronged test, based on the NLRA, for determining whether given business entities are deemed a single employer for labor law purposes.[10] The four elements of this test are:

1. common ownership of the entities,

2. common management of the entities,

---

[8] *Id.,* 29 U.S.C. § 160(1).

[9] For a thorough examination of the legislation, NLRB rulings, and court decisions on secondary boycotts, *see* Ralph M. Dereshinsky, Alan D. Berkowitz, and Philip A. Miscimarra, *The NLRB and Secondary Boycotts,* 2nd ed., Labor Relations and Public Policy Series, No. 4 (Philadelphia: Industrial Research Unit, The Wharton School, University of Pennsylvania, 1981).

[10] *See* Radio & Television Broadcast Technicians Local 1264 v. Broadcast Service of Mobile, Inc., 380 U.S. 255, 256 (1965) *per curiam, quoted with approval* in South Prarie Construction Co. v. Local 627, IUOE, 425 U.S. 800, 802 n.3 (1976).

3. integration and interrelation of entity operation, and

4. centralized control of labor relations.

In evaluating whether a single employer relationship exists, the NLRB and the courts weigh all four of the above factors. Of the four, the most important is whether the entities have common or centralized control of labor relations.[11] Analysis of this issue turns on the existence of actual and active day-to-day centralized control of labor relations,[12] not on potential centralized control of labor relations. Because the potential costs of being a single employer are so high and the distinctions between a single employer and separate employers are imprecise, employers planning to operate during a strike are best advised to examine their organizational relationships and seek legal counsel with respect to any possible single-employer problems that might arise.

Publicity Boycotts. Striking unions may pressure consumers to boycott the products of a company with which they have a dispute after the products are in the hands of a neutral employer.[13] Nevertheless, although they may publicize their dispute, they may not by picketing urge customers to boycott a totally neutral employer that uses or carries a product of the struck employer.[14] A consumer boycott initiated by striking employees falls outside the protection of the law if (1) it results in refusals by employees, other than those of the struck employer, to pick up, to deliver, to transport goods or to perform services, or (2) the publicity is untruthful.

A neutral employer may be subject to a consumer boycott if the company being struck has at some stage produced, in the sense of applying capital, enterprise, or services, a product of the neutral employer.[15] This standard has been construed extremely broadly.[16] Yet one court has held that this standard does not sanction a boycott against an entire conglomerate when only one division is being struck and the con-

---

[11] *See* NLRB v. General Teamster, Warehouse and Dairy Employees, Local No. 162, 435 F.2d 288, 291 (7th Cir. 1970); Gerace Construction Co., Inc., 193 N.L.R.B. 645, 650, n.9 (1971).

[12] *See* Carpenters District Council of Houston, 201 N.L.R.B. 23, 26 (1973).

[13] NLRB v. Fruit and Vegetable Packers Local 760, 377 U.S. 58 (1964).

[14] NLRB v. Retail Store Employees Union, Local 1001, 447 U.S. 607 (1980); Kroger Company v. NLRB, 647 F.2d 634 (1980).

[15] *See* NLRB v. Servette, Inc., 377 U.S. 46 (1964); Great Western Broadcasting Corp. v. NLRB, 356 F.2d 434 (9th Cir.), *cert. denied*, 384 U.S. 1002 (1966).

[16] *See, e.g.,* Florida Gulf Coast Building Trades Council, 252 N.L.R.B. No. 99 (1980), *enforced sub nom.* Edward J. DeBartolo Corp. v. NLRB, 108 L.R.R.M. 2729 (4th Cir. 1981), where the court ruled that other stores in a shopping mall could be boycotted, as they derived a benefit from the presence of an incoming store that was being struck, because it employed a nonunion contractor.

glomerate is organized in totally independent operating units.[17] In addition, picketing to induce a consumer boycott violates section 8(b)(4)(ii)(B) if a successful boycott is "reasonably likely to threaten the neutral party with ruin or substantial loss."[18] Thus, a union cannot engage in consumer picketing of a neutral employer that depends on the products of the primary employer for most of the neutral employer's business.

Customer and supplier relations received considerable attention in the operating plans and preparations of most of the firms studied, but that attention generally did not focus on the possibility of a supplier or customer boycott. Instead, most firms assumed that they would be able to do business as usual and so attempted to assure customers and suppliers. There was little in the accumulated experience of the companies studied to suggest that they seriously underestimated the possibility of an adverse reaction of suppliers or customers to the decision to operate.

The only fairly consistent problem encountered with either suppliers or customers was reluctance to send their personnel and equipment through picket lines to deliver or pick up goods, although even that problem was far from universal. This problem typically was solved by moving goods into or out of the plant through the use of company personnel and equipment. On several occasions, this involved "smuggling" goods into or out of the plant in the trunks of the cars of nonstriking employees. In one case, it involved the use of a hose to smuggle in fuel oil from a neighboring distributor that refused to risk crossing a picket line with its own trucks.

There were virtually no reports of reluctance on the part of suppliers to do business with a struck facility because it continued to operate. One company did report an instance in which a local firm that supplied the company with the cots and blankets required to house nonstriking personnel in-plant informed the company that it would not be willing to do so in the future because of its concern about the reaction of its other customers. A second company had a somewhat similar experience when it found that its plea for the support of the local business community in encouraging an end to a strike fell on deaf ears because of fears of "customer reaction" against any merchant who took a position on the issue.

Instances of problems with customers were even more rare. One company did report some concern on the part of one customer about the willingness of its employees to process products received from the

---

[17] Pet, Inc. v. NLRB, 641 F.2d 545 (8th Cir. 1981). *Contra,* Edward J. DeBartolo Corp. v. NLRB, 108 L.R.R.M. 2729 (4th Cir. 1981).

[18] NLRB v. Retail Store Employees Union, Local 1001, 447 U.S. 607, 615 n.11 (1980).

struck plant, but that concern proved groundless and resulted in no interruption of business. No other company reported a similar problem with the employees of its customers or suppliers. Nor was there any report of a consumer boycott of the struck company's products or those of a customer arising out of plant operation.

The lack of boycott pressures on the firms studied may be attributed to the fact that they typically were relatively immune to all but secondary boycotts, which are subject to both legal and practical limitations as a potential union power asset. Thus far, those legal and practical limitations appear to have discouraged attempts by unions to use boycotts as a counterweapon to plant operation. Unions have tended, instead, to look to government regulatory agencies such as OSHA and the Environmental Protection Agency (EPA) as more accessible and willing allies in making it difficult for companies to operate during strikes. The potential power of such regulatory agencies to interfere with operation was more awesome to most employers than the power of unions to achieve the same end through pressure on customers or suppliers.

THE ROLE OF INJUNCTIVE RELIEF

The ultimate weapon against mass picketing and picket line violence is injunctive relief to secure free access to the plant. For those companies that were unwilling to breach the picket line, injunctive relief was their only weapon to lift the siege. Not surprisingly, these companies tended to weigh the prospects for such relief most heavily in the decision to operate. The companies that were willing to cross the picket line did not weigh injunctive relief as heavily in deciding to operate, but were no less interested in judicial action as a means to ensure unhindered access.

Legal Parameters of Injunctive Relief

The legal parameters of injunctive relief were outlined above in Chapter II. Essentially, state law usually forbids violent, intimidating, or coercive conduct by employees engaged in an otherwise lawful strike. Examples of illegal conduct include (1) mass picketing, (2) blocking of ingress or egress, (3) violence or threats of violence against customers or nonstriking employees, and (4) interfering with common carriers.

The specific facts of each case determine whether an injunction will be issued. An employer must present evidence that the misconduct it seeks to prohibit has occurred, is likely to recur if not prohibited, and will thereby cause irreparable damage. Further, a company must generally assert that, despite efforts to do so, the police have not been able to provide adequate protection for those attempting to cross the picket line and/or for the employer's business. How effective the injunction issued will be in prohibiting the conduct under question will depend on the strength of the evidenced presented; therefore, the employer must establish a procedure whereby all such evidence is collected and prepared for presentation in court.

Company Activity to Secure Evidence for an Injunction

As explained in Chapter II, an employer must exercise caution in the collection and preservation of evidence to obtain an injunction because interference with, restraint of, or coercion of employees engaged in an economic strike is prohibited under section 8(a)(1) of the NLRA.[19] Without proper justification, photographing or otherwise monitoring picket line activity can be construed by the NLRB to be illegal activity.[20]

An employer may justify surveillance of the picket line on the grounds that it is gathering evidence to obtain an injunction to halt illegal activity.[21] If no such activity has yet occurred, an employer must be able to substantiate its anticipation of violence or other unlawful strike activity with objective evidence, such as misconduct in other strikes engaged in by the union.

The pursuit of injunctive relief to limit picketing activity was an integral part of the operating plans of every company in the sample. Those plans focused on the steps to be taken to secure the evidence necessary to support a successful request for injunctive relief. Thus, all of the strike plans contained elaborate provisions for observing and recording incidents of picket line violence. The plans included the following:

1. Maintenance of a chronological log of all pertinent activity by pickets and striking employees;

2. continual observation by local staff employees familiar with the names of striking employees;

3. collection of sworn statements from company employees and other individuals who are victims of or witnesses to picket line incidents; and

4. collection of photographic evidence: still photos, movies, and videotape.

---

[19] 29 U.S.C. § 158(a)(1).

[20] *See* Puritana Manufacturing Corp., 159 N.L.R.B. 518, 519, n.2 (1966).

[21] *See* Excavation-Construction, Inc., 248 N.L.R.B. No. 81 (1980).

Photographic records of picket line incidents are the best evidence for securing the attention of the court. Still photography generally does not have the same impact as action photography in conveying the true character of picket line activity. The two alternatives for action photography open to management are motion pictures and television videotape. The first option is less expensive in terms of capital investment, and is less productive in terms of its practical value. Specifically, videotape has two important advantages over motion pictures that justify its use:

1. Videotape does not require developing, thereby permitting a company to be in court in the afternoon on the basis of the morning's activities and incidents.

2. Videotape can be erased and reused.

The Use and Limits of Injunctive Relief

For nearly every strike, the sampled companies were compelled to seek the aid of the courts to establish or to facilitate access to their struck plants. In clearly unusual cases, companies reported that the combined efforts of the union, the company, and the local law enforcement officials had been sufficiently effective in maintaining order on the picket line to make an injunction unnecessary.

In the experience of the companies surveyed, injunctive relief was far from automatic. As explained above, this was in part because of the proof required to document union misconduct. Whether injunctive relief is secured may also depend on more than legal argument. For example, the political setting in a particular state may be a crucial variable. States with high concentrations of organized labor are likely to tolerate higher levels of confrontation on the picket line and may be less inclined to grant injunctive relief, or at best be inclined toward narrow injunctions.

Obtaining injunctive relief restricting picket activity clearly represents a legal victory for management. Nevertheless, the extent of that victory is heavily dependent on the specific scope and wording of the injunction. Injunctions may contain general prohibitions against unlawful conduct, but they may also be more specific and restrict the conditions under which picketing may occur. For example, courts have limited the number of pickets to counter mass picketing and its resultant blocking of access to an employer's premises when that has been shown.[22] Because they tend to reduce the potential for disruptive

---

[22] *See, e.g.,* International Molders and Allied Workers Union, Local 164 v. Superior Court, 70 Cal. App.3d 395, 406, 138 Cal. Rptr. 74,800 (1977).

conduct and because violations of them are easier to prove, specific restrictions are often more effective than general prohibitions.

Most of the companies studied felt that their interests had been adequately protected by the judicial restraints on picket activity. One company, for example, was able to get an injunction that banned all picketing for the two one-half-hour periods that coincided with shift changes. Several companies, however, indicated that their interests had not been well served by the scope of the injunctive relief. Included among these companies was one for which a judge conditioned a ban on mass picketing on the proviso that all those entering the plant should roll down their windows to ensure that they would be able to hear the striking workers' side of the story.

The practical significance of management's victory in securing injunctive relief depends on the effect of the injunction on the willingness and ability of the union and its members to exercise self-discipline in their conduct on the picket line. Companies rarely perceived no positive self-enforcement effects at all, but similarly they saw few cases in which the self-enforcement effects were immediate and dramatic. Specifically, several companies indicated that temporary restraining orders had relatively little calming effect in their own right or in comparison with permanent injunctions. Nonetheless, temporary restraining orders generally appeared to force a measure of self-discipline on unions and workers.

The effectiveness of an injunction ultimately depends on more than the willingness of the enjoined party to accept voluntarily the court-imposed restrictions on its actions. An injunction's effectiveness is determined by the willingness of local law enforcement agencies to enforce its terms and the employer's willingness to bring contempt proceedings if those terms are not obeyed.

The experiences of the sampled companies indicated that access to law enforcement agencies for enforcement of injunctive relief was subject to the same political realities that were found to affect the courts issuing relief, as was discussed above. Nevertheless, and not surprisingly, the companies also observed that law enforcement agencies became more willing to become involved in a labor dispute once injunctive relief was granted.

Plainly, although injunctive relief played a crucial role in the operating plans of all of the companies sampled, seeking such relief entails certain risks. If an injunction is sought and denied, the union or employees may construe that as a form of approval and may be encouraged to continue or to increase their activities. If a weak injunction is issued, it may well be ineffective. Because of these factors, an employer must be all the more concerned about ensuring that all evidence of misconduct is gathered, preserved, and put in the proper form for use in court.

The timing of seeking an injunction is critical. Seeking an injunction before major problems have arisen can lead to either the denial of injunctive relief or the issuance of an order that fails adequately to provide the protection required in operating the facility. Care must also be taken to ensure that any injunction issued is in compliance with state laws governing the issuance of injunctions. Failure to comply with state laws can lead to the injunction being vacated and to the employer paying the costs of such an action.

SUMMARY

An employer that elects to operate during a strike must expect a determined effort by striking workers to inhibit the movement of personnel and product into and out of a struck facility. The basic weapons available to workers in such an effort are picketing and other means of publicizing the existence of a labor dispute that are designed to persuade individuals not to do business with the struck facility. In addition to ordinary picketing and publicity, striking workers can be expected to utilize devices such as mass picketing and boycotts to dissuade those inclined to continue to do business with an employer despite the existence of a labor dispute.

The battle to gain or maintain access to a struck plant is fought primarily at the plant perimeter. Mass picketing is a common phenomenon in plant operation situations and is the most formidable challenge facing an employer that elects to operate. Thus far, striking workers and unions generally have not extended their efforts to inhibit access to nonstruck facilities, suppliers, customers, or the community of the struck facility. The fundamental reason for this relatively narrow focus on the immediate site of the labor dispute appears to be the statutory ban on secondary boycott activity. The scope of that ban is imprecise, but unions thus far have not been willing to test its limits in plant operation situations, to the benefit of those employers that have elected to operate.

The most significant problem created by the efforts of striking workers to inhibit access to a struck facility is a refusal by unionized employees of the struck employer and other employers to cross the picket line. Thus, any employer that elects to operate must be prepared to do so without the services of such employees. This is not a trivial problem because the workers in question typically are skilled or licensed personnel who are not easily replaced. The most prevalent and troublesome problem in this respect is the refusal of unionized transport personnel to cross a picket line.

The battle to gain or maintain access is one in which employers have an often reluctant ally in the courts. In general, operating employers have been able to secure injunctive relief against those picket line activities that most severely impede access. That relief is not automatic and may not be easy to secure, but typically is available to any employer that needs it and is prepared to demonstrate that need. Through careful preparation, most employers have been able to do so. Thus, state law regulating conduct of picketing activity, like federal law regulating conduct of boycott activity, has proven to be important, if not essential, in giving practical meaning to the right of an employer to operate during a strike.

CHAPTER VI

The Logistics of Operation: Security

The decision to operate a plant during a strike, if implemented successfully, threatens to undermine the union's basic power asset in collective bargaining—the strike. Because unions and unionized workers are unlikely to be sanguine about such a threat, management must expect that the union and its members will utilize a wide range of tactics to make successful plant operation as difficult as possible.

Picketing is the most common tactic used to inhibit plant operation, but it is not the only device used to that end. Harassment of individuals who continue to do business with the struck plant is not uncommon in plant operation situations. Sabotage of physical facilities is another possibility that cannot be ignored. Thus, a company that decides to operate must be prepared to deal with such tactics and to provide for the security of essential personnel and physical plant facilities.

HARASSMENT

One possible union response to plant operation is intensified efforts to dissuade individuals from providing the goods and services that the struck employer needs to operate. These efforts may involve implied threats or explicit acts of violence directed at nonparticipants in the strike. Such threats or acts may take place either at the plant site in the form of picket line violence or away from the plant site in the form of personal intimidation. They may be directed at either nonstriking company employees or employees of other employers servicing the struck plant.

Picket Line Violence

Emotional encounters on a picket line are common even in the event of nonoperation, but are far more likely in the event of operation. They were typical in the case of the firms studied. Emotional encounters often escalate beyond the hurling of insults to threats against those attempting to enter a struck facility. Vandalism of vehicles, as described in the previous chapter, also is not uncommon, particularly

87

when an employer aggressively seeks to gain or to maintain access to a struck facility. Occasionally, this vandalism escalates to overturning or burning vehicles or physically removing or abusing vehicle occupants. Incidents of this type have not been widespread in any situation of plant operation among the companies studied, but many firms reported isolated cases of such activity in a number of their plant operating experiences.

The vulnerability of personnel to harassment, vandalism, and possibly physical violence typically diminishes dramatically once they are inside the plant perimeter. It may not, however, totally disappear. A plant perimeter may be breached by rocks, bullets, or other missiles such as ball bearings fired by slingshot. Several firms reported isolated instances of such activity, but most perceived that it was aimed more at plant windows than plant personnel, and only a few reported actual injury to personnel as a result of such activity. A plant perimeter may also be breached by individuals determined to cause problems. Incursions of this type were extremely rare in the experience of the companies studied. One firm, however, did report a case in which a supervisor was beaten at a remote part of the site at night, and another reported a case in which a guard station was stormed and its occupants beaten.

Minor picket line violence or other strike misbehavior is to be expected given the contentious nature of strikes.[1] The NLRB and the courts have been highly tolerant of emotional encounters on the picket line. The NLRB has provided a standard for determining whether strike misconduct warrants discharge:

> [T]he applicable test in determining whether strikers accused of misconduct should be returned to work "is whether the misconduct 'is so violent or of such serious character as to render the employees unfit for further service,' or whether it merely constitutes 'a trivial rough incident' occurring in 'a moment of animal exuberance.'" This distinction has been drawn on the theory that some types of "impulsive behavior," being "normal outgrowths of the intense feelings developed on picket lines," "must have been within the contemplation of Congress when it provided" for the right to strike.[2]

The Board has ruled that "mere threats"[3] or obnoxious conduct[4] are insufficient by themselves to justify the termination of a striker. But when threats are coupled with some overt physical act suggesting

---

[1] *See* NLRB v. Hartmann Luggage Co., 453 F.2d 178 (6th Cir. 1971).

[2] Huss & Schlieper Co., 194 N.L.R.B. 572, 577 (1971).

[3] *See* W.C. McQuaide, Inc., 220 N.L.R.B. 593 (1975), *modified,* 552 F.2d 519 (3d Cir. 1977).

[4] *See* Ohio Power Co., 215 N.L.R.B. 165 (1974), *modified,* 539 F.2d 575 (6th Cir. 1976), where a striker plucked a cigar from a supervisor's mouth and threw it to the ground.

a willingness or ability to make good on the threat, an employer may discharge the employee or refuse to reinstate him.[5]

If an employee is unlawfully terminated, he is entitled to back pay from the date of his termination. Under some circumstances, a wrongful termination could convert a strike into an unfair labor practice strike,[6] thus entitling the striking employees to reinstatement to their former jobs upon making an offer to return to work.

Self-Help Measures against Picket Line Violence

The ultimate weapon of an employer against harassment, vandalism, and violence generally is injunctive relief and local law enforcement authorities. Because the protection afforded by such remedies is not automatic and may not totally deter such activity, employers that elect to operate generally prepare to take self-help measures, at least to a limited extent. Three types of self-help measures can and have been taken by companies that operate: preventive, remedial, and deterrent (in the form of discipline or discharge).

Preventive Measures. The most common and effective self-help measure taken to prevent the exposure of personnel to harassment, vandalism, and violence on the picket line has been the housing of nonstriking operating personnel on-site, as discussed in the previous chapter. Less common and effective has been the use of convoys of cars or buses. The problem of protecting employees on-site involved first and foremost efforts to secure the plant perimeter against intruders through a combination of fencing, lighting, and security patrols—measures routinely taken by firms that operate, with apparently excellent results overall. The problem of protecting personnel from harassment by verbal or physical "sniping" from outside the plant perimeter generally can be accomplished by physical isolation of working personnel from the plant perimeter using buffer zones. When this is not feasible, other measures can be taken, as exemplified by a newspaper that permanently bricked up all of its windows facing the street before a strike began, and by a chemical company that moved its personnel out of a plant administration building near the plant perimeter until all of its windows had been shot out, as inevitably happened. All firms instructed working personnel not to approach the

---

[5] *See, e.g.,* NLRB v. Moore Business Forms, Inc., 574 F.2d 835 (5th Cir. 1978) (no reinstatement of employees who placed nails in a road, threw eggs at cars, or threatened an employee's family); W.J. Ruscoe Co. v. NLRB, 406 F.2d 725 (6th Cir. 1969) (no reinstatement of employees who rocked a car and blocked its ingress into a plant, or threw gravel at a photographer); Oneita Knitting Mills, Inc. v. NLRB, 375 F.2d 385 (4th Cir. 1967) (no reinstatement of employees who threw eggs at cars).

[6] NLRB v. International Van Lines, 409 U.S. 48 (1972).

picket line except when absolutely necessary and not to engage in discussions or debates with pickets at any time.

Remedial Action. The combination of effective preventive measures, injunctive relief, and law enforcement can dramatically limit harassment, vandalism, and violence on the picket line, but may not totally eliminate those phenomena. A second line of defense against the disruptive effects of these problems is remedial action. Employers generally make it clear to nonstriking employees that the company is ready to compensate them for damage to their vehicles not covered by their own insurance that results from crossing a picket line. Although the situation rarely arises, two firms have provided financial and legal support for supervisory personnel in challenging fines imposed on them by their unions for crossing a picket line. Firms have also sought damages from unions for acts of vandalism. One firm obtained $35,000.00 from the striking union as part of a final contract settlement to cover the cost of replacement of windows smashed during a strike.

Individual employees also may be able to recover damages for injuries sustained from strike violence. Individuals have recovered damages under state tort law and under the Civil Rights Act of 1871 (the Ku Klux Klan Act).[7] For example, as mentioned in Chapter II, in the recent case of *Boyd v. Russell*[8] an Arkansas state court concluded that the union defendants in a strike evidence case had engaged in a "deliberate, outrageous, malicious campaign to abuse, threaten and harass the plaintiffs," and awarded those plaintiffs $250,000 in damages on the basis that such action constituted a tortious intentional infliction of emotional distress. In another case, *Scott v. Moore,*[9] all of the unions in an area building trades council were enjoined and assessed damages for a violent mob action against a nonunion employer and its employees on a construction site under the Civil Rights Act of 1871 (the Ku Klux Klan Act).

Discipline and Discharge as Deterrents. The right of an employer to discipline or discharge strikers for unlawful picket activity constitutes a potentially powerful deterrent to such activity among even the most emotional and zealous of striking workers.

Exercise of the right to discipline striking workers for actions taken on a picket line can create both legal and practical problems for an employer. Legally, an employer that exercises this right must be able to prove to an arbitrator and/or the NLRB that the actions that were

---

[7] 42 U.S.C. § 1985(3).

[8] No. 78-488 (Cir. Ct. Garland City, Ark., July 7, 1980).

[9] 640 F.2d 708 (5th Cir. 1981).

the basis for discipline were indeed committed by the individual disciplined and that those actions were unlawful, unprotected, and sufficiently grave to justify the discipline imposed. Practically, an employer that exercises this right is likely to find that its actions have created a whole new set of issues to be resolved in achieving an agreement to end the strike. Specifically, there was unanimous agreement among the companies studied that disciplinary action taken against striking workers would lead to demands that such action be rescinded or modified as part of any strike settlement.

In the face of these potential problems, a majority of the companies studied chose not to make extensive use of their right to discipline as a self-help deterrent to harassment and vandalism on the picket line. In electing this policy, practical rather than legal considerations played the primary role. Although confident in their ability to discern the legal limits on their disciplinary rights, most companies were unwilling to defend that action at the bargaining table. Specifically, most firms chose not to be aggressive in disciplining striking employees except in extreme cases because they realized that such action was likely to be rescinded or modified as the price of ending the strike. Such concessions were perceived to have two significant adverse tactical effects for the company: (1) nonstriking personnel who were the targets of the actions in question were likely to feel that the company had sold them out; and (2) striking workers were likely to conclude that they had little to fear from the company for misconduct on the picket line.

A minority of companies did pursue aggressive discipline policies. Included among these firms were most of those that also aggressively sought to gain and maintain access. Those firms believed that they could not expect nonstriking employees to run the gauntlet of the picket line without some clear demonstration that the company supported their struggle.

The same tactical and morale considerations that dictated relatively aggressive use of discipline also dictated relatively aggressive resistance to union demands for lifting disciplinary penalties as part of a strike settlement. One firm, however, has taken the opposite approach: it has adopted an informal practice of "firing one striker per day" in order both to diminish the enthusiasm of those on the picket line and to increase the number of "silver bullets" it has available to offer at settlement time. That firm has stated that it has had no serious morale problems among nonstriking personnel as a result of this practice, but it also has admitted that it spends considerable effort in explaining its approach and building an understanding of the role of the "will to lose" in the collective bargaining process.

Personal Intimidation

Attempts by striking workers to disrupt the flow of personnel and product into and out of a struck plant need not be confined to a picket line. Actions to dissuade individuals from aiding or serving an employer that elects to operate take place away from the plant site as well as at the site. These actions most often concern nonstriking, replacement employees, but also may extend to workers in the employ of outside suppliers of goods and services.

Most of the companies studied reported that in almost all of their operating experiences there were acts of harassment and vandalism directed at the families and homes of salaried personnel serving as replacement workers in a struck plant. The number and nature of such acts varied widely from situation to situation. None of the firms indicated that personal intimidation was widespread or well-organized, and most cited harassing phone calls to the homes of nonstriking employees as the most prevalent act of attempted intimidation. Also noted with some consistency were acts of vandalism directed at the homes of nonstriking employees, most notably the throwing of eggs or paint. A few firms reported isolated instances of more serious acts of vandalism. These acts included the sabotage of cars, boats, and campers stored at home and even more serious acts of violence, such as the firing of shots or throwing of fire bombs at the homes of employees and attempts to run employees down or force them off the road.

These acts of off-site harassment, vandalism, and violence generally were perceived by the companies studied as the work of a small group of "hotheads" and "troublemakers" whose anger and frustration did not stem from the company's decision to operate but undoubtedly was exacerbated by that decision. Several firms perceived an upward trend in personal intimidation over time during plant operation, suggesting that anger and frustration grow and spread as a strike drags on and it becomes increasingly apparent to striking workers that the company is operating the struck facility with reasonable success. This view was supported by the perception of other firms that the importation of outside company personnel or hiring of replacements typically resulted in acts of personal intimidation. In a few cases, the issuance of effective injunctions limiting picket line activity were viewed as having led to off-site intimidation by forcing the hotheads and troublemakers to seek other avenues to vent their anger and frustration.

Although personal intimidation of employees and their families reportedly was not a prevalent tactic of striking workers, it admittedly posed a serious problem for management. The ability of an employer to operate depends on the commitment of those individuals assigned to strike duty. That commitment may actually be strengthened by acts of intimidation occurring at the picket line, perhaps because it is managerial rather than supervisory or clerical personnel who are usually the primary targets of such acts. The same is not necessarily the case, even among managerial personnel, for acts of intimidation directed at the home and family of a nonstriking employee.

The problem of off-site personal intimidation is not limited to nonstriking company employees. It can extend to those who do business with a struck plant—most notably to those who drive trucks carrying company cargo. The vulnerability of trucks and their drivers to intimidation on the open road is obvious, as has been demonstrated in the case of steel haulers. Several firms reported that incidents of attempted harassment and vandalism of trucks carrying their cargo have occurred well outside the plant perimeter. Other suppliers of goods or services to a struck plant may be subject to the same type of activity, but it is their trucking contractors and personnel who have borne the brunt of union intimidation in the experience of the companies studied.

Remedies for Intimidation

The legal remedies for personal intimidation are the same as those available in cases of picket line violence but generally are far less readily available and effective than in the case of picket line activity. A company may terminate or discharge employees when it can prove that they have engaged in serious or aggravated misconduct,[10] but this is a burden that is likely to be difficult if not impossible to bear in the case of what may be sporadic, scattered, or even random instances of off-site harassment, vandalism, and violence. An employer also may seek injunctive relief against acts of personal intimidation on- and off-site. The burden of proof, however, will be heavy, and if secured, the injunctive relief is likely to be ineffective in preventing intimidation attempts.

A union may be found liable for the acts of its striking members if the company can prove union direction and knowledge.[11] Recently unions have been found liable under alternative theories of law. The Teamsters were found to have violated the Travel Act[12] and the Racketeer Influenced and Corrupt Organization Act (RICO)[13] by using

---

[10] *See, e.g.,* NLRB v. Moore Business Forms, Inc., 574 F.2d 835 (5th Cir. 1978) (an employer was not compelled to reinstate employees who had threatened nonstriking employees by saying "There's ways to keep you from [going to work]," and had threatened the family of another nonstriking employee).

[11] *See, e.g.,* Compton v. Puerto Rico Newspaper Guild, Local 225, 343 F. Supp. 884 (D.P.R. 1972); Local 248, Meat & Allied Food Workers, 222 N.L.R.B. 1023 (1976), *enforced,* 84 Lab. Cas. (CCH) ¶ 10,826 (7th Cir. 1978).

[12] 18 U.S.C. § 1952.

[13] 18 U.S.C. § 1962(d).

explosives to damage trucks in interstate commerce, by crossing state lines to commit arson on the company's trucks, and by conspiring to conduct union affairs (an enterprise) through a pattern of racketeering (the various violent acts).[14] The standard of proof in these actions is rigorous, but in certain circumstances, legal action against the union may force it to control its members more closely.

Other recent case law has suggested additional weapons available to management and its employees to counter intimidation efforts. Though not a well-established option in the case law, nonstriking employees who are targets of intimidation may sue the individuals who commit such acts for the intentional infliction of emotional distress, as in *Boyd v. Russell.*[15] Or, as in *Scott v. Moore,*[16] an employer and its employees may take action against the unions involved in violence against them.

The limited accessibility and effectiveness of judicial remedies for acts of off-site personal intimidation basically leave an employer at the mercy of law enforcement agencies for the control of such acts. In most cases, those agencies were judged to have been relatively cooperative and responsive in dealing with off-site personal intimidation problems—more so than in the case of similar problems on-site created by picketing activity. Only one firm reported that police were reluctant to cooperate in an off-site setting; they intervened only after paint was mistakenly thrown at the homes of "innocent citizens." The general willingness of police to deal with off-site intimidation is in marked contrast to the reports of police reluctance to become involved in labor disputes at the site of such disputes until an injunction has been issued. In most cases, off-site intimidation has not been sufficiently extensive to overtax the capability of law enforcement agencies to the point at which such activity has gotten out of control.

No employer need be totally at the mercy of police protection to control and deter off-site intimidation. Although no firm can provide physical protection for a large number of employees and their families outside the plant site, most can do so for a limited number of its key personnel and their families, if necessary. Only a very few of the companies studied, however, actually felt compelled to take such action. One firm reported that it had offered bodyguards and family vacations to specific individuals in some isolated situations, but indicated that its offers generally were not accepted. A second firm provided twenty-four-hour protection for two of its key supervisory personnel and their families, and a third reported hiring off-duty police officers to augment local police in patrolling specific areas in the local community in which

---

[14] United States v. Thordarson, 646 F.2d 1323 (9th Cir. 1981).

[15] No. 78-488 (Cir. Ct., Garland City, Ark. July 7, 1980).

[16] 640 F.2d 708 (5th Cir. 1981).

the residences of managerial and supervisory personnel were concentrated. A far more substantial number of companies reported private security efforts to control or deter acts of intimidation against personnel driving trucks carrying company cargo. These efforts ranged from having observers armed with a camera ride along to hiring private security personnel to serve as escorts.

SABOTAGE

A second possible response of workers to the decision to operate is to sabotage plant and equipment. Sabotage has been prominently reported in plant operation situations, but little is known of its overall incidence and significance in such situations. There can be little doubt, however, that sabotage can be a potentially powerful counterweapon to the exercise of the right to operate by management—a fact recently noted by at least one union. In this context, it is important to distinguish two types of sabotage: (1) prestrike sabotage—steps taken by workers prior to a strike deadline to create problems for the company in taking over or starting up operations with nonstriking company personnel; and (2) poststrike sabotage—actions taken by workers while on strike to make it technologically more difficult for the company to operate with replacement personnel.

The law clearly allows an employer to discharge employees who commit sabotage[17] if the employer can prove that the specific employees actually committed the violent act(s).[18] If the sabotage is extremely widespread and very serious, then the actions by the employees may be viewed as an in-plant strike, thus allowing the employer to permanently replace the entire work force without identifying specific wrongdoers.[19] For this right of general discharge to accrue to an employer, the employees' actions must essentially deny the employer the benefit of its employees' energies and the employer's action must be free of antiunion animus.[20]

---

[17] *See* Seminole Asphalt Refining, Inc. v. NLRB, 497 F.2d 247 (5th Cir. 1974) (the company was permitted to discharge employees who threw cherry bombs into the vicinity of company petroleum storage tanks).

[18] *See* Methodist Hospital of Kentucky, Inc. v. NLRB, 619 F.2d 563 (6th Cir.), *cert. denied,* 449 U.S. 889 (1980); NLRB v. Big Three Industrial Gas & Equipment Co., 579 F.2d 304 (5th Cir. 1978), *cert. denied,* 440 U.S. 960 (1979).

[19] Johns-Manville Products Corp. v. NLRB, 557 F.2d 1126 (5th Cir. 1977), *cert. denied sub nom.* Oil, Chemical & Atomic Workers International Union v. Johns-Manville Products Corp., 436 U.S. 956 (1978). *But see* American Cyanamid Co. v. NLRB, 592 F.2d 356 (7th Cir. 1979), where the company was held liable for substantial lost earnings for taking actions similar to those taken by the employer in *Johns-Manville.*

[20] NLRB v. Big Three Industrial Gas & Equipment Co., 579 F.2d 304 (5th Cir. 1978), *cert. denied,* 440 U.S. 960 (1979). *See also* Methodist Hospital of Kentucky, Inc. v. NLRB, 619 F.2d 563 (6th Cir.), *cert. denied,* 449 U.S. 889 (1980).

Most acts of sabotage also violate state criminal laws. A company, therefore, may both discipline and criminally prosecute employees caught committing sabotage.

Because most employees who commit such acts are judgment-proof, an employer action in tort to recover damages is likely to be futile. Nevertheless, the filing of such a suit could send an important message to the employees regarding the seriousness of the company in such matters.

Prestrike Sabotage

The ability of workers to "throw monkey wrenches into the works" at any time is not open to question. The willingness of workers generally to utilize this power is extremely limited but may not remain so in the face of pending union-management confrontation. The prospect that the union may not fare well in that confrontation because of management's commitment to operate during a strike may create an added incentive to engage in sabotage prior to a strike. A union faced with that same prospect may encourage or at least tolerate such actions among its members.

The possibility of prestrike sabotage was a real concern of virtually all of the companies studied. The basic defense of the companies against this possibility was very close supervision of workers during the final prestrike shift coupled with an "escort to the gate" at the end of the shift. A few firms, however, took the added precaution of having managerial and supervisory personnel take over operations at the start of the shift immediately preceding the contract deadline. The practices of these companies with respect to the bargaining-unit personnel scheduled to work the final shift included: (1) instructing workers not to report, (2) sending workers home early, and (3) having workers sit out their shift in the cafeteria. In all such cases, workers were paid for the full shift in order to avoid charges of a lockout.

Overall, the level of prestrike sabotage reported by the operating companies was surprisingly low and not significantly different from what might be expected prior to a strike in which there was no threat of operation. Only one firm indicated that it had experienced systematic, serious prestrike sabotage in any of its plants, and that problem was largely confined to one plant. One other firm indicated that prestrike sabotage generally was a problem, but not one of major proportions. The remaining companies typically reported either no problems or only isolated minor problems with it. The incidents reported by these firms generally were not particularly subtle, devious, or dangerous and were attributed to the work of isolated, disgruntled employees.

The limited incidence of prestrike sabotage may have been a function of the precautionary measures taken in anticipation of the problem. Most of the companies, however, also credited the self-discipline of workers and unions as a factor. This self-discipline, in the view of several of the companies, could be traced to the perception of workers that their jobs depended on the continued operational capability of the existing plant and its equipment; they were unwilling, therefore, to take actions that might seriously impair that capability.

Sabotage during a Strike

The possibility of sabotage does not end with the exit of bargaining-unit members from the plant. However secure a plant may be by virtue of fencing, lighting, and security patrols, it is always possible for a determined individual to penetrate the plant perimeter, particularly where that perimeter stretches for several miles. Outside that perimeter, the vulnerability of a company to sabotage increases dramatically.

The companies studied were no less concerned about their vulnerability to sabotage after than before a strike began. This was evident in the routine steps taken to secure plant perimeters in preparation for a possible strike and to augment security forces once a strike began. A special concern of virtually all of the companies was the vulnerability of their links to utilities and their remote site facilities because they were outside the protection of the plant perimeter. Generally, it is not feasible to secure all such linkages and facilities, but most firms routinely prepare to observe or patrol the most obvious points of vulnerability.

For most of the companies studied, sabotage during a strike was a far more serious and prevalent problem than sabotage prior to a strike. Nearly all of the companies reported at least one major sabotage attempt in conjunction with each of their major plant operation efforts. In no case, however, did the number of such attempts approach what was perceived to be "epidemic" proportions. In no case were such attempts sufficiently effective to cause the company to contemplate ceasing plant operation.

A number of companies reported bomb or arson threats against an operating point. In one case it was only the timely appearance of the state police that deterred a group of pickets from implementing their stated intent of setting fire to the plant administration building. In most instances, these threats proved idle and were designed only to harass the company and possibly disrupt operations. One firm was the target of an apparent bombing attempt. In that case, several sticks of dynamite with a charred fuse were found outside the plant power house. The police concluded, however, that the fuse had been burned before it was attached to the dynamite.

The relative immunity of plant sites to acts of sabotage during strikes has not extended to facilities located outside the plant perimeter. Several companies sustained substantial damage at their remote sites— damage that in one case totalled about $250,000.00. Most companies reported incidents of sabotage directed at their links to utilities and supplies of raw materials. The most prevalent form of such sabotage was the cutting of telephone lines, a contingency for which most companies routinely prepared. Less common, but more serious, were attempts to cut off electrical power by severing power lines, shorting out substations and transformers, or, in one case, dynamiting a major power-line tower. Two companies reported attempts to sabotage or shut off water supplies. Four others reported that pipelines carrying raw materials or finished products were dynamited or cut. One firm reported an attempt to burn a bridge on the railroad siding serving its plant.

Although such acts of sabotage clearly are not a welcome part of plant operation, they are seemingly an inevitable part of it. Recognizing that fact, most companies have prepared to deal with the possible consequences of sabotage. Thus far, all have been quite successful in coping with it during strikes. None have significantly curtailed operations as a result of sabotage. Nonetheless, that possibility continues to concern many companies, some of which are constantly seeking ways to "strike proof" further their facilities.

The success of companies in coping with sabotage during a strike, as with sabotage prior to a strike, is the result not only of their own preparations but also of the self-discipline of most workers. None of the companies studied perceived a systematic campaign to sabotage operations during a strike, and all expressed the view that the acts of sabotage they did experience were the work of a few extremists acting alone and out of frustration or desperation. Even for these individuals, sabotage apparently is not a preferred course of action, as acts of sabotage tend to occur only after it is evident that a plant is operating successfully and may be able to do so indefinitely. Moreover, acts of sabotage tend to be concentrated off-site, where risk of detection is lower, as is the risk of long-run impairment of the operational viability of the plant.

SUMMARY

After problems of recruiting manpower and maintaining plant access, the third major challenge facing an employer that decides to operate during a strike is the protection of the physical safety of those persons and facilities whose services are required to sustain production. The potential for violence exists in the emotions aroused by any strike, and that potential can only be enhanced by a decision to operate during a strike. Thus, an employer that makes that decision must anticipate threats or acts of violence directed at both personnel and facilities that continue to serve the employer during strike operations. Specifically, an employer must be prepared to deal with attempts by striking workers to intimidate nonstriking personnel, either on the plant site, off the plant site, or, most notably, at the plant perimeter and to sabotage physical facilities, either prior to or during a strike.

Harassment of nonstriking company personnel is a common phenomenon in plant operation situations. The most prevalent forms of such activity are vandalism and violence on the picket line. Almost equally common, but far less prevalent, are incidents of vandalism or violence aimed at nonstriking personnel beyond the picket line at home or on the road. Intimidation attempts on the plant site are rare but have been known to occur.

Sabotage, like harassment, is not uncommon in plant operation situations, although it has proved to be far less widespread and extensive in overall incidence. On-site sabotage either before or during a strike rarely has been a problem that companies have not been able to prevent. Off-site sabotage or sabotage at the plant perimeter, as in the case of harassment and intimidation, has been a serious problem for employers attempting to operate, although generally not prior to or at the outset of a strike. Thus far, that problem has not proven unmanageable primarily because sabotage has rarely been formally endorsed by unions or informally sanctioned by workers.

Acts of intimidation or sabotage that occur on the plant site are subject to a considerable measure of direct control and restraint by an employer. Similar acts committed on the picket line are subject to at least a limited measure of direct employer control through its right to discipline striking workers for provable picket line misconduct supported by its ability to observe picket activity in search of proof of such misconduct. Beyond the picket line, however, acts of intimidation and sabotage are far more likely to escape effective direct observation and control by an employer, thereby forcing the employer to rely on the vigilance and responsiveness of the police and the courts for control of such acts. To date, this external line of defense generally has proven adequate to the task of coping with sporadic, isolated acts of intimidation and sabotage committed by a few hostile, frustrated individuals. Whether it would prove adequate against an extensive, systematic campaign of intimidation or sabotage remains an unanswered question.

CHAPTER VII

The Willingness to Operate: Economic Considerations

By operating during a strike an employer can limit the loss of revenue and profit associated with a temporary cessation of production. Specifically, plant operation can limit loss of sales in the short run and loss of customers in the long run. The avoidance of such losses may be important in its own right but must ultimately be justified by a favorable short-run or long-run impact on profit or loss—revenue minus cost. Thus, one basic set of questions regarding the logic of plant operation involves the extent to which it has been effective in limiting loss of sales and customers and has been a cost-effective means of accomplishing that end.

Plant operation is one of three ways in which an employer can limit loss of sales and profit as a result of a strike. The other options, noted in the planning guidelines of all of the companies studied, are inventory buildup and transfer of production. Each of these options has its own advantages and limitations in cutting losses due to a strike. In theory, those firms that have elected to operate must have concluded that plant operation was the most cost-effective means to limit strike losses. In practice, however, companies did not formally analyze the relative effectiveness of plant operation in limiting losses of profits due to a strike. Thus, the economic logic of plant operation has been a matter of subjective judgment rather than objective proof.

MARKET POSITION

All of the companies studied were convinced that their efforts to operate during strikes had been highly worthwhile in terms of avoiding losses of sales in the short run and customers in the long run. There was considerable variability among the companies in the extent to which plant operation was successful in avoiding short-run loss of sales. There was, however, consistent emphasis that plant operation served to avoid long-run losses of customers by maintaining the reputation of the company and plant as a reliable source of supply.

That many firms cited continuity of relationships with major customers as a primary economic benefit of plant operation is not surprising given the problems likely to confront a firm in maintaining normal operations while using replacement personnel. It does, however, raise the question of whether employers operating during a strike are vulnerable to primary or secondary consumer boycotts designed to undermine such customer-supplier relationships.

Because only a few of the companies studied were themselves engaged directly in the production of consumer goods, most were largely immune to direct consumer boycott pressure. Although none of the firms would be totally immune to secondary consumer boycott pressure directed at them through their customers, none have yet been subjected to such pressure or experienced any clear reluctance on the part of major customers to continue to do business with a struck plant.

Maintaining Sales

The ability of an employer to limit loss of sales in the short run through plant operation will be determined in large part by the level of production achieved by replacement personnel. None of the companies studied planned to operate at 100 percent of normal capacity during a strike. Most attempted to build an inventory to supplement planned production in the event of a strike. Most firms did not contemplate transfer of operations as a supplement to operation. A few, however, did consider such action after a strike had been underway for a considerable length of time. One firm was forced to consider leasing a plant to which it might transfer some of its struck operations.

Production Rates: Full Operation. A number of firms reported that their production goals for struck plants typically were 80 to 90 percent of normal capacity. These firms generally were those operating capital-intensive, continuous-process production facilities of the type found in oil refining, utilities, and parts of the chemical industry. These firms typically were able to meet or exceed even ambitious production goals. One firm, which began strike operations with the modest goal of 75 percent of normal production, soon exceeded that goal by a substantial margin. Two companies indicated that they had no difficulty in maintaining production at rates in excess of 90 percent of normal capacity. Two other companies reported setting new production records during strike operations, one on a daily and weekly basis and the other on a monthly basis.

These firms obviously experienced no significant loss of sales as a result of a strike. Most did admit some loss of sales as a result of customer "hedging" against the possible effects of a strike. This hedging disrupted not only production but also shipping operations. Most firms sought to limit hedging by assuring customers that they would operate and ship during any strike, but few firms claimed to have been totally successful in that effort. Overall, however, these losses plus the loss of 5 to 10 percent of production capacity were not perceived to have involved a serious loss of sales and revenue for the companies in terms of either their short-run or long-run position.

Production Rates: Partial Operation. A second group of firms operated with less ambitious production goals, in the range of 50 to 80 percent of normal capacity. These partial operation companies typically were engaged in production operations that were only semicontinuous and more labor-intensive than those of their full operation counterparts. The scope and focus of partial operation were determined by both technological feasibility and economic necessity. Specifically, within the limits of technological feasibility, the partial operation firms concentrated on key products that were either basic to the company product line, especially profitable, or vital to the needs of major customers. In any event, these firms generally aimed to operate at 80 to 100 percent of normal capacity for their key products, which typically meant an overall plant operation at between 50 and 75 percent of normal capacity.

Most of these firms were able to meet their basic, partial operation production goals, but often only with the assistance of company personnel from other locations and, in some cases, outside replacements. None reported setting new production records or exceeding production goals. Many admitted that they had been pleasantly surprised by achieving even their partial operating goals. All of these firms indicated that they had lost sales and revenues notwithstanding their efforts to operate, but all asserted that plant operation had limited the magnitude of such losses in terms of the long-run market position and profitability of the company. That is, most believed that, although the strike cost them sales in the short run, their ability to keep key products on the market through partial plant operation enabled them to limit such losses and avoid losses of their most important sales to important customers.

Production Rates: Limited Partial Operation. A third group of plants found only very limited partial operation to be feasible. These plants typically were highly labor-intensive and could not be operated at even 50 percent of normal capacity without more extensive use of replacement labor than was available within the company or local labor market, absent a return-to-work movement. The basic operating goal in these situations was to finish work in progress or to produce essential parts to meet the most pressing needs of a limited number of major customers. These limited operation plants were reasonably successful in meeting their modest production goals during strike operations and in averting potentially catastrophic losses of sales and customers. Although catastrophic sales losses were thus avoided, "non-catastrophic" sales losses were considered significant. One company reported that it had not missed a shipment to its major customers during a strike, but also admitted that it had contemplated opening a new plant as a result of the competitive pressure exerted on it by that strike. Another company reported that its customers generally were understanding of delays in filling orders but also mentioned that it had been compelled to consider the use of permanent replacements as a means to alleviate such delays.

Retaining Customers

Virtually all of the companies indicated that their operation during a strike had lasting favorable effects on their relations with customers. Once firms had demonstrated their ability to accept and fill customer orders throughout the course of a strike, customers were reported to be far less anxious about the effects of a possible strike on their supply of materials, less likely to shift orders to alternative suppliers, and more understanding and tolerant of minor delivery delays and longer lead times.

The long-run customer relations benefits of plant operation were not automatic: they had to be cultivated by the operating company. Most companies went to considerable lengths to assure customers of their intent to operate should a strike occur and to reassure customers of their ability to operate once a strike was underway. This was not an easy task for most firms in their initial plant operation experiences. One plant lost 50 percent of its market share as the result of a strike despite its efforts to operate for the first time. The task became easier once the company had demonstrated its ability to operate successfully, but never so easy that customers could be taken for granted. Thus, customer relations inevitably received close attention in preparations for operation and continued to receive such attention during the course of plant operation.

Companies routinely notified customers of the possibility of a labor dispute and of their intention to continue to meet the needs of their customers should a labor dispute indeed occur. When necessary or appropriate, firms also worked closely with their major customers prior to a possible strike in an effort to coordinate customer needs with the operational capacity of a struck facility. Finally, all firms took steps to build a sufficient inventory off-site to assure customers of continuity of supply during the initial stages of a strike, when direct shipments from a struck facility could be expected to be most difficult.

Plant operation typically requires a curtailment of normal sales and service activities, but not a complete elimination of such activity. Thus, firms and facilities generally are prepared to continue to provide sales service to major customers on demand. In addition, all firms take measures to maintain quality-control activities during strike operation and to inform customers of those measures. In some cases product quality standards actually were raised during strike operations to minimize the risk of problems with major customers. Overall, in virtually all operating situations the quality of product was reported to be less of a problem than the quantity of product in meeting the needs of customers.

Product delivery, like product quality, is a major concern of customers of a facility operating during a strike. Customers typically understand the problems of shipping products from a struck plant but are willing to be tolerant only to a limited degree. The responsibility for solving this problem basically falls on the struck facility. Few customers will offer, as the U.S. Army did in the case of one plant, to come and get their merchandise, picket line or no picket line. Most customers, however, are willing to accept delivery by alternate transportation modes or routes, when necessary, as long as the struck facility absorbs any additional freight costs. Many companies have had to make these alternate transportation arrangements to serve their customers during strike operations.

FINANCIAL CONDITION

The varying degrees of success that operating firms have enjoyed in maintaining sales and retaining customers suggest that plant operation has enhanced both the short-run and long-run revenue of those firms in terms of what those revenues would have been in the case of nonoperation. Plant operation, however, is not a costless undertaking. It may, therefore, not have a comparably favorable effect on the short-run profits or long-run profitability of the plant. Specifically, to guage the economic merits of plant operation, the incremental revenue generated by plant operation must be weighed against the short-run incremental costs and long-run opportunity costs of the resources utilized to operate a plant during a strike.

The costs of plant operation, like its benefits, were not quantified by the companies studied. Virtually all of those companies, however, asserted that plant operation had been financially worthwhile in the short run in cutting some of the profit loss that otherwise would have occurred as a result of a strike. Most companies recognized that there might be some long-run sacrifice of profits inherent in the diversion of resources required to operate a plant during a strike, but none believed that such a sacrifice was significant in terms of the long-run profitability of the plant or company.

Short-Run Performance

The prospect of a strike threatens a plant not only with a loss of profit but also with the possibility of a negative profit. That negative profit is attributable to the fixed costs that the plant must assume whether or not it operates. Elements of fixed cost include taxes, depreciation, corporate overhead, and the salaries of nonstriking personnel. If, through plant operation, a firm can use the resources represented by those costs to generate revenues, it may be able to limit or eliminate its negative profits associated with a strike. The magnitude of such fixed costs in most industries constitutes a potentially powerful economic incentive to attempt plant operation. Thus, it is not surprising that several of the companies studied specifically cited as an economic benefit of plant operation the fact that production during strikes enabled them to recoup some of the costs of overhead.

Plant operation, per se, does not guarantee a cut in the losses associated with a strike, even when using only existing company resources. Ignoring for the moment any possible opportunity costs of diverting resources from their normal use to the operation of a struck facility, the incremental costs of that use of resources can be substantial. Included among such incremental costs are the cost of vandalism and violence; the cost of overtime premium pay; and the cost of importing, housing, and feeding company personnel assigned to strike duty. Most firms did not provide data on the extent of these incremental costs, but virtually all admitted that they could be substantial. Despite the magnitude of the incremental costs of operation, all firms asserted that operation had enabled them to cut their strike losses significantly. One firm claimed that operation of one of its large plants during a strike added $25 million to reported corporate profits for the year.

Overall, the experiences of the companies studied suggest that, in the short run, it is more expensive to operate using replacement personnel than normal personnel but less costly to operate using replacement personnel than not to operate at all. For most plants, including those which reported high quantity and quality of output using substantially fewer replacements than normal, the incremental costs of operating during a strike were sufficiently great to prevent the plant from making a greater than normal profit on units of output. Thus, no firm reported having done better than to "break even" with respect to profit margins during strike operations, and most were not even willing to claim that they had done that well. Nonetheless, all believed that the positive, if limited, profit margins on strike production were a significant factor in limiting the adverse effects of strikes on reported corporate profits.

Long-Run Profitability

The apparent short-run financial and marketing benefits of plant operation must be weighed against the opportunity costs inherent in the diversion of resources from their normal use to the operation of a struck plant. These costs constitute a potentially significant hidden cost of operation, the ultimate effect of which may be to reduce the long-run profitability of the enterprise in question.

The use of management personnel as production labor clearly is not the optimal use of that human resource. Most importantly, it inevitably requires some curtailment of managerial activities and functions. All of the companies studied were aware of this problem, but none had attempted to measure its magnitude or assess its long-run significance. Most reported that all basic managerial functions were continued during strike operations, but at 50 percent or less of normal staff and activity levels. All claimed that such reduced staff and activity were sufficient to carry on essential day-to-day managerial functions, but all of the companies studied admitted that such managerial functions as anticipating future problems or planning long-run strategies had to be ignored during operation.

Similarly, the use of process and product development personnel as production workers involves some loss in the development of new technology and product. This sacrifice was particularly noticeable because research and development functions typically were totally shut down to free personnel for strike duty. Once again, all companies were aware of this cost of operation but did not perceive the temporary suspension of research and development activities during the period of strike operation as a serious threat to the future profitability of the firm. Indeed, some claimed that the use of research and development personnel in strike operations enhanced the long-run effectiveness of that activity by providing those personnel with a better understanding of the actual conditions in which their ideas have to be implemented.

Finally, the use of sales personnel as production workers clearly involves some curtailment of efforts to develop new sales and customers, as well as efforts to serve existing customers. Most firms sought to provide at least limited service to existing customers, but virtually all had to curtail or suspend efforts to find new customers. There was unanimous agreement that this involved a potential loss for the company, but most of the firms argued that any loss could be limited or avoided by compensatory efforts after the strike ended. Those firms that used clerical personnel for strike duty perceived and managed the problems associated with that action on much the same terms.

While most firms appeared able to cope with their most pressing day-to-day managerial, sales, and clerical problems during strike operation, the cost of their failure to address other problems and lost opportunities during the strike remains undetermined. Most companies admitted that attention to long-run problems and lost opportunities had been deferred until after the strike had ended. The companies generally assumed that the cost of this delay and of the effort required to catch up on deferred work was minor—an assumption that, although open to question, is difficult to test.

There can be little doubt that plant operation entails opportunity costs that have an adverse effect on long-run profitability. It is also possible, however, that plant operation may create offsetting permanent improvements in productivity. Most companies were as anxious to discuss such long-run benefits of plant operation as they were reluctant to discuss the potential long-run costs of plant operation.

The major reported long-run economic benefit of plant operation was increased operating efficiency. Virtually all of the companies reported that they made permanent changes in manning as a result of their experience in operating with nonstriking personnel. These changes resulted in manning reductions of as much as 15 to 20 percent in some large plants after an initial operating experience. In most cases, however, the reductions were more modest, on the order of 3 to 5 percent. One firm, as a matter of policy, has a goal of effectuating reductions in manning of at least this magnitude in every operating situation.

Several firms suggested a second long-run efficiency effect of plant operation: improved morale and understanding within the ranks of company nonunion personnel. The sense of camaraderie and team membership developed in the shared exhilaration and pain of strike duty was perceived by a number of companies as having had a subtle long-run positive impact on the commitment and productivity of nonunion company personnel at all levels. Similarly, most firms felt that management, by actually working in the plant, gained a better understanding of production problems, leading to more effective communication and cooperation between management and production personnel over the long run.

SUMMARY

The basic economic goal of a company operating during a strike is to limit its short-run losses of sales and profits and long-run losses of customers and profitability. In theory, plant operation could not only limit such losses, it could actually eliminate them. In practice, however, even firms that are highly successful in operating struck facilities at or near normal capacity have not been able to achieve this ideal result. Thus, at best, plant operation is a means to cut losses owing to a strike.

Plant operation has proven to be an effective means to limit losses of sales and particularly customers. For a few companies blessed with highly capital-intensive production facilities, the saving of sales and customers has approached 100 percent. For most companies, however, such savings have been far more modest and confined to sales of key products or sales to key customers. Not even those companies able to operate at nearly normal levels of production were able to continue to do business as usual, either with respect to serving their existing customers or cultivating new customers. Thus, in terms of market position, plant operation is, at best, a holding action.

Although plant operation enables firms to reduce the loss of sales and customers, its direct incremental costs—particularly for firms that attempt to operate at better than 50 percent of normal capacity—typically are sufficiently great to prevent any plant from making a short-run profit. For most, however, plant operation has substantially reduced short-run losses. That reduction has been purchased at the largely intangible and unmeasurable price of lost managerial, engineering, sales, and clerical services—a sacrifice that arguably should have an adverse impact on long-run profitability. That sacrifice, however, appears to have been at least partially offset by long-run productivity improvements initiated during plant operation.

Overall, the sales and profit benefits of operating apparently equal or exceed the economic costs associated with it. The evidence is not clear, however, that the cost-benefit rationale for plant operation is superior to similar ratios for other approaches to limiting strike losses (such as inventory accumulation) or is competitive with rates of return normally expected on the investment of corporate resources. Thus, although plant operation may be justified solely on the basis of immediate considerations of market position and financial condition, the potential labor relations benefits that may stem from a successful attempt to operate are equally important considerations.

The Willingness to Operate: Institutional Considerations

The fundamental effect, if not purpose, of plant operation is to alter the balance of economic power in collective bargaining in management's favor by limiting the loss of revenue and profit resulting from a strike. In the short run, this enhanced bargaining power should enable management to secure a more favorable settlement of strike issues than would have been the case in the event of nonoperation. In the long run, this enhanced bargaining power should result in a series of more modest settlements, possibly to the point of seriously weakening the perceived effectiveness of a union or unions generally in representing employees. Such management "victories," however, are not likely to be won easily. They may have to be won at the price of increased tension, if not bitterness, in both employee and union relations, both immediately after a strike and over the long run as workers and unions vent whatever frustration they experience as a result of management's enhanced bargaining power.

BARGAINING POWER

The right of an employer to take a strike over mandatory bargaining issues rather than accede to union demands is management's most basic and potent weapon in collective bargaining. An employer that is both willing and able to operate during a strike should be more willing and better able to take a strike than an employer that either will not or cannot operate. The effect of this enhanced willingness and ability to take a strike, and particularly a long strike, should be to reduce the gains likely to be won by the union through strike action. Thus, the immediate effect of operation should be to force a reappraisal by the union of its likelihood of prevailing because of its strike action. The result may be an enhanced willingness on its part to seek and accept compromise on strike issues. Over the long run, the proven commitment of an employer to operation should enhance the credibility of its implicit or explicit threat to take a long strike, thus resulting in more moderate settlements with fewer and shorter strikes.

The Short Run

Most of the firms studied believed that their decision to operate a production facility enabled them to achieve a more favorable settlement with the union at that facility than would have been possible absent operation. None of the firms put a price tag on the concessions secured or avoided as a result of operation, but most felt that their gains had been substantial and sufficient to offset the incremental and opportunity costs of operation. Avoidance of concessions on issues of principle such as management rights, work rules, and cost-of-living escalators, which are inherently difficult to price, often was cited as a major benefit of operation.

The best gauge of an employer's ability to prevail in a test of economic power is the extent to which it succeeds in making its final prestrike offer the basis for the ultimate contract settlement. The records of the employers studied with respect to this test varied widely but basically fell into three categories.

1. Firms that were able to achieve a high level of output during a strike typically were able to base their final settlement on their last prestrike offer, but not without some symbolic concessions— "silver bullets"—most often in the form of dropping charges or rescinding disciplinary action against some individual strikers.

2. Firms that were able to sustain only partial operation typically were able to secure settlements within the overall limits of their final offer, but only with some rearrangement of that offer plus a few silver bullets of the type noted above.

3. Plants that were able to maintain only limited operation typically found it necessary to add to as well as to rearrange their final prestrike offers in order to achieve a settlement, but not without some comparable compromise on the part of the union.

Settlements, regardless of their character, generally were not effected quickly or easily. Plant operation, per se, typically had little or no immediate impact on the militancy of either striking workers or their union. Whatever psychological effect plant operation might have on striking workers was not evident at the outset of a strike. In many cases, this lack of immediate psychological effect was attributed by employers to the fact that strikers did not believe that the plant was operating successfully—a belief often encouraged by their unions. The conviction that management was only "sending up steam" and "sending out empty trucks" was most prevalent in initial operating situations or in operating situations involving large plants, but was by no means confined to such situations.

The only apparent cure for worker/union skepticism regarding management's ability to operate is the passage of time. The reluctant realization that the plant indeed is operating typically produces an escalation of efforts by a minority of striking workers to impede operation. For the majority of striking workers, however, that realization apparently forces a reappraisal of their expectations regarding the outcome of strike action. The result generally is increased union interest in returning to serious negotiations to resolve the deadlock.

The return to serious negotiations, however, typically did not produce a settlement in short order, even in those relatively few situations in which there was some evidence of an emerging back-to-work movement. These negotiations generally opened with little or no change in the position of either party and proceeded to closure only with considerable difficulty. Several firms reported having to make two or three alternative settlement and return-to-work offers before achieving an agreement. One reported that even after several months such an agreement was reached only as a result of a "call to Washington."

The difficulty of achieving a settlement even after it has been established that operation has been successful can be attributed to the fact that operation adds little to the level of pain experienced by striking workers as opposed to the expected duration of that pain. In that context, the apparently increasing willingness and ability of workers to undertake prolonged strikes constitutes a problem for employers that operate as well as for those that do not, although clearly not of the same economic magnitude. The only device open to management to enhance the level as opposed to the duration of pain is its policy on prosecution and discipline for acts of violence. Aggressive disciplinary action by an employer can create an institutional problem sufficiently ominous to force the union to seek and accept a settlement based on a trade-off of "silver bullets" (discipline) for "silver bullion" (economics). Such a trade-off is not without its problems from the viewpoint of management, but most firms are willing to accept a limited measure of such problems in exchange for an economically advantageous settlement and return to normal operations.

The ultimate management weapon in enhancing the level of pain experienced by striking workers is the hiring of permanent replacements. Several companies in the sample brandished or actually used this weapon, with varying results. Typically, the mere announcement of the intent to hire replacements produced little or no manifest increase in worker or union interest in achieving an expeditious settlement, primarily because of worker and union skepticism regarding the ability of any employer to hire strikebreakers. In some cases, the announcement of the intent to hire accompanied by the taking of applications and the hiring of the first few replacements was sufficient to dispel that skepticism and propel the union into a settlement. In other cases, the hiring of permanent replacements had to proceed quite far before the attitudes of strikers and their union changed sufficiently to permit a settlement. Finally, in a few cases, the process was completed without inducing a settlement.

Because the holding power of workers and unions in the face of plant operation and the possibility of permanent replacement constitutes an important union power asset, only those employers that were able to operate at high levels of output over a protracted period of time using permanent replacements, if necessary, were truly able to claim victory at the bargaining table. Those employers whose capacity to operate was limited with respect to level or duration of production and that did not hire replacements to enhance their capacity to operate had to settle for something less under the weight of current or prospective strike losses.

The Long Run

The proven willingness and ability of an employer to operate during a strike should enhance the credibility of its implicit threat of a long and unsuccessful strike in any future bargaining impasse. The result should be greater reluctance on the part of workers to resort to strike action and more interest in compromise and accommodation at the bargaining table, at least until they can implement actions to limit the employer's desire and capability to operate.

Deterrent Effect of Operation

Most of the companies studied reported that plant operation did have some effect on worker and union militancy beyond the specific operating situation. Few firms, however, were willing to claim that such effect was either profound, pervasive, or long-lasting. Thus, the threat of operation, like the threat of a strike, has its limits in forcing peaceful accommodations in collective bargaining.

Only a very few firms felt that their demonstrated commitment to operate a specific plant had any manifest moderating effect on union demands in subsequent negotiations at that plant. Most companies, however, perceived that operation did diminish enthusiasm for a strike in support of those demands at least in the next set of contract negotiations. Beyond that set of negotiations, however, the deterrent effect of the implicit or explicit threat of operation tended to weaken, although it rarely disappeard judging by the frequency with which unions raised the subject in negotiations. The weakening of the deterrent effect was most rapid and evident in those plants that had not operated long or well in their previous effort. It was those plants that were the most likely, but not the only, plants to report multiple operating experiences within an eight- to ten-year period.

The effect of plant operation on union and worker militancy at other plants of a company was even more modest. None of the companies were willing to claim that their success in operating one plant provided them with any manifest bargaining leverage in another of their plants that had no recent history of operating during a strike. There were a few exceptions to this pattern among firms with sufficiently visible and extensive plant operation experience to have gained a reputation for their commitment to plant operation, but even they had to prove that commitment more than once and at more than one plant.

It is not surprising that the willingness and ability of an employer to operate, like the willingness and ability of an employer to take a strike, must be proven on more than one occasion and in more than one bargaining relationship. In the adversary environment of collective bargaining, threats are always likely to be suspect; the threat of operation is no exception. The credibility of that threat is a function of the recentness and results of actual prior experience. It may also be tempered by a basic reluctance on the part of workers and unions to accept the fact that management can successfully counteract their basic weapon—the strike—leaving them all but powerless in that process.

Changing the Status Quo

The apparent reluctance of workers and unions to accept the long-run bargaining power implications of successful plant operation may explain why workers and unions have not yet actively sought to change the status quo. With very few exceptions, workers in the companies studied have not tried to decertify their bargaining representatives as a result of strikes rendered ineffective by plant operation. Similarly, unions have not sought new weapons to inhibit the willingness and ability of employers to operate. For the most part, the employers studied have not encouraged the former type of change in the status quo, perhaps out of fear of encouraging the latter type of change. Indeed, most employers studiously avoid any explicit reference to the potential impotence of a union and strike action in dealing with unionized employees, although they do not show a similar reluctance to discuss the futility of unionization and strike action in dealing with non-unionized employees.

The fairly sanguine response of employees and employers to the potential change in relative bargaining power inherent in successful plant operation undoubtedly is an important factor in explaining the equally sanguine response of most unions to plant operation in the companies studied. The fact that successful plant operation can serve to undermine the basic weapon of a union in collective bargaining suggests that unions cannot passively accept operation indefinitely, particularly in light of the growing intent and capability of the companies studied to operate during strikes. Thus, it is logical to anticipate efforts by unions to find new ways to inhibit the willingness and ability of employers to operate. The nature of such efforts remains to be seen, but two general possibilities should be noted: (1) government intervention through new legislation or interpretation of existing legislation; and (2) self-help measures such as sabotage, sympathy strikes, and coalition bargaining.

Government Intervention. The prospect for government intervention to assist unions in inhibiting employers from operating during strikes is not imminent primarily because plant operation is not a management tactic that is sufficiently widely used to attract national attention. The body of law that protects the right of an employer to operate, to hire replacements, to maintain ingress and egress, and to utilize company personnel to operate a struck facility seems sufficiently well-rooted to be an unlikely candidate for legislative limitation. Also remote is the possibility of a modification of the statutory ban on secondary labor boycott activity. The body of regulations, which thus far have constituted more a bother than a barrier for employers that elect to operate, also seem unlikely to become dramatically more bothersome in the immediate future. Nevertheless, the possibility of NLRB rulings or OSHA regulations that might severely complicate plant operation continues to concern a number of employers committed to plant operation.

Self-Help Measures. There are a number of self-help measures legally available to unions in attempting to inhibit exercise of the right to operate. One union countermeasure is the right to initiate consumer boycotts—a right that the labor movement is just beginning to exploit on a serious basis. Two other possibilities are sympathy strikes at other company plants and coalition bargaining, either of which could be used in an attempt to overtax the ability of a company to operate during strikes. Thus far, such cooperative strike action has not been a major problem for the companies studied because decisions to operate one plant have not elicited supportive militancy or strike action in other company plants, even when such action has been actively sought by the striking union and would have coincided with contract negotiations at other plants. The possibility of such concerted action, however, was a source of concern for a number of the companies studied. One firm felt compelled to prepare to operate at least a dozen plants simultaneously in response to a major coalition effort by one of its major unions.

There are two other possible extralegal, self-help measures open to unions that thus far have been relatively little explored or exploited. The first is sabotage, particularly prestrike sabotage. That possibility has been and remains a serious concern of most employers committed to operation but has not proven to be a major or growing problem for most such employers. The second is the organization of supervisory personnel in order to control their availability for strike duty. To date, few unions have had much success in such organizing efforts, although some have had success in organizing other potential sources of in-house replacement personnel, such as technical and clerical workers. Unions may also seek other indirect means to control the use of supervisory personnel for strike duty. One firm recently found itself confronted with a demand by one of its unions to bargain over the promotion of its members to the position of temporary supervisor to replace supervisors assigned to strike duty at another company plant.

Overall, the long-run experience of the firms studied suggests an uneasy acceptance of plant operation as a management power asset in collective bargaining. Thus far, there has been no clear tendency toward an escalation of conflict or power. Most managements have not pressed whatever power advantage they have gained as a result of plant operation, and most unions have not been able to find the means to rectify whatever power disadvantages they have experienced as a result of plant operation. The restraint of management is a matter of tactical choice. The restraint of unions in plant operation situations may simply reflect their lack of power. In the situations studied they have lacked the visibility and clout to command the sympathy and cooperation of the government, the labor movement, other unions, and, in some cases, even their own international union in attempting to discourage or inhibit plant operation. Thus, they have been essentially left to their own devices—tenacity and, to a lesser extent, violence—in responding to the challenge of plant operation. The situation is likely to remain that way unless plant operation threatens to produce a far more profound and pervasive change in the basic balance of bargaining power in labor-management relations than it has yet done.

BARGAINING PROBLEMS

The decision to operate in the short run and the commitment to operate in the long run involve a clear escalation of conflict as well as of power in union-management relations. The escalation of conflict by management may well elicit a similar escalation of conflict by a union and its members in their relations with management. Specifically, it is likely that plant operation will engender bitterness on the part of unionized workers and their union toward management, which will adversely affect their working relationships over the long run. Any deterioration in working relationships should be most evident upon a return to work following a strike but may persist and become a permanent part of the day-to-day relationship between the union and management.

The Short Run

Most of the companies studied admitted that there was a "coolness" in their relationship with unions immediately following the end of strikes. This coolness generally was acknowledged to be more pronounced than would be expected in a situation in which a plant did not operate during a strike. In no case, however, was this coolness perceived by management to involve a serious breakdown in working relationships. This was true even when the hiring of permanent replacements had been initiated, although one such firm did indicate that its poststrike relations with the union had been sufficiently hostile to induce management to take steps to establish a basis for a more cordial relationship.

None of the firms were willing to admit that the same coolness spilled over into the shop floor on any significant scale, although most would admit that a few employees, most often those subjected to discipline for picket line misconduct, harbored some resentment. All of the firms reported little personal animosity on the part of employees toward those supervisory and managerial personnel who had served as their replacements during a strike, although one firm did indicate that its plant strike coordinators often were the target of poststrike animosity. Two explanations were offered for this lack of poststrike bitterness: (1) workers accepted the argument that keeping the plant operating helped preserve their jobs over the long run; and (2) workers understood that managers and supervisors worked out of necessity rather than choice. This same understanding did not extend to replacements hired during and retained after the strike.

Animosity among Supervisory and Managerial Personnel

The lack of animosity on the part of returning workers toward supervisory and managerial personnel was not always reciprocal. A number of firms perceived that some supervisory and management personnel took an adversarial attitude toward employees on their return to work. Many reported "morale problems" among victims of strike-related harassment, intimidation, and violence when they learned of management's decision to drop legal charges or disciplinary actions against some strikers as part of a contract settlement. The potential for this attitudinal problem was sufficiently great and widespread to induce most firms to instruct supervisory and other personnel on the welcoming of returning workers.

The attitudes and morale of supervisory personnel pose a dilemma for management in plant operation. On the one hand, the development of a strong will to win among this group of employees who must work longest and hardest if the plant is to operate is crucial to building the morale and commitment required to achieve a high level of operation. On the other, this same adversarial attitude becomes a potential liability once it is possible to resume normal operations.

This attitudinal dilemma creates another dilemma for management in the development and implementation of policy on disciplining strike misconduct. Discipline of striking employees is one obvious way in which an employer can signal its own will to win and willingness to support supervisory personnel. If it chooses to send this signal, however, it risks disillusioning those personnel when it is necessary to have the will to lose in order to achieve a settlement. The solution to this disciplinary dilemma pursued by most firms was to distinguish two types of transgressions. To prove the company's commitment to and support of its supervisory personnel and other victims of strike-related violence, it would rigorously discipline or prosecute a few employees who committed serious transgressions and then refuse to negotiate these cases. The cases of employees disciplined for less serious offenses would be negotiated and could be conceded as silver bullets to achieve a settlement, but not without careful explanations of the reasons for such action for the benefit of nonstriking personnel.

Overall, the problem of poststrike bitterness, like the problem of prestrike sabotage, appears to be limited in scope. Most firms were concerned about potential problems associated with the return to work after operation just as they were with potential problems associated with the departure from work prior to operation, more so than they would be absent exercise of the right to operate. Most firms carefully prepare to deal with return-to-work problems as they do with departure-from-work problems. For the most part, they have been as successful in avoiding the former as they have been in preventing the latter.

The Long Run

The philosophical and practical commitment to plant operation of most of the companies studied has placed them in a long-run "power bargaining" relationship with their unions. Just as it seems reasonable to anticipate a union response to the escalation of power inherent in this type of bargaining relationship, so too is it reasonable to expect a union response to the escalation of conflict associated with power bargaining. To the extent that management is able to gain and maintain a bargaining power advantage through plant operation, it is unlikely that contract negotiations will serve as a primary vehicle for escalation of conflict by a union. There are, however, other avenues open to a union to escalate conflict, including the narrow world of contract administration and the broad arena of public opinion, political pressure, and government regulation.

There is no sound basis on which to determine the extent to which the companies studied have been subjected to an escalation of conflict outside contract negotiations as a result of their commitments to plant operation because there are no norms against which to judge their experience. For example, most firms did not believe that plant operation resulted in a significantly higher grievance and arbitration case load over the long run, although few would discount that possibility completely. Similarly, most firms did not believe that they had been the target of a disproportionate number of unfair labor practice charges, OSHA inspections, or other regulatory or legal actions over the long run as a consequence of plant operation, although few could convincingly refute that possibility. Finally, most asserted that they had not been subjected to extraordinary political pressure or public exposure over the long run as a result of plant operation, an assertion which defies empirical test.

The question of whether the firms studied have been subjected to a significant escalation of conflict as a result of their decisions to operate remains open. The potential for such an escalation of conflict, however, is not open to question. There is ample evidence of the vulnerability of any company, whether it operates or not, to harassment or embarrassment by a union through court suits, regulatory complaints, or wildcat strikes or other protest actions conducted in the name of worker safety or community welfare. There also is every reason to believe that a union that is party to a power bargaining relationship will be less reluctant to avail itself of such opportunities than one that is party to an "accommodation bargaining" relationship in which management is unwilling to operate during a strike.

SUMMARY

Plant operation provides employers with the means to limit short-run and long-run strike losses not only in the marketplace but also at the bargaining table. The limitation of losses at the bargaining table often has been an important factor in the willingness of employers to operate and typically is cited as a major benefit of plant operation. The most visible dimension of this benefit is economic and involves the cost and efficiency savings realized at the bargaining table as a result of plant operation. The more subtle, but potentially equally significant, dimension of this benefit is institutional and involves the acquisition of enhanced power and control in union-management relations.

The ability of an employer to limit the economic cost of a strike through plant operation serves to enhance its willingness to take a strike. The result typically has been more favorable settlements than would otherwise have been possible. Seldom, however, have those settlements come quickly or easily, primarily because of a fundamental skepticism on the part of striking unions and workers regarding companies' ability to operate and willingness to take a long strike. The extent to which such skepticism has been justified in terms of limits on the ability of a plant to operate at near normal capacity has determined the extent to which management has been able to prevail in the settlement of issues in dispute.

CHAPTER IX

Conclusion

The employer's right to continue to do business in the face of a strike by operating its production facilities with temporary or permanent replacement workers is clearly recognized under law. This right is qualified by an extensive set of federal, state, and in some cases, local regulations governing various aspects of bargaining and employment relationships. At this time, however, those regulations, while potentially bothersome, are not a real barrier to the exercise of the right to operate.

Although the right to operate during strikes provides employers with a weapon to augment their right to take a strike in the conduct of collective bargaining, to date that weapon has only seldom been used; it has not become a basic part of the American system of collective bargaining. The chief exception to this rule is that of plant operation in a few high-technology industries, most notably the oil, chemical, and telephone industries. There is, however, evidence to indicate that this situation may be changing, as shown by a growing number of widely publicized instances of plant operation by firms in other industries that previously had not operated and in which operation had seemed infeasible.

The limited exercise of the right to operate is not difficult to explain. The logistical problems of securing an adequate supply of replacement labor to operate a struck facility, coupled with the problems of moving personnel, materials, and the product through picket lines tend to deter any attempt to operate. Equally imposing are the potential institutional problems associated with plant operation, most notably worker or union violence in the short run and retribution in the long run.

The logistical problems of operating a plant during a strike and the fear of failure to which they give rise constitute a formidable but not insurmountable barrier to operation. These problems are rarely solved easily and are never solved well without extensive preparation, but with such planning a growing number of firms have found these problems to be manageable. Indeed, most firms that have chosen to confront these problems have found them to be even more manageable than originally anticipated, leading them to expand the scope of their attempts to operate during strikes. The conclusion they draw from their own experience is that the fear of failure is rational but easily overdrawn, at least prior to an initial operating attempt.

The key to the success of firms in managing the logistical problems of operating during a strike has been their ability to recruit an adequate supply of replacement labor. The determinant of success in this respect, in turn, has been their ability to rely heavily or exclusively on managerial, supervisory, and other nonunion company personnel rather than on either a return-to-work movement among striking personnel or the hiring of replacements in the external labor market. As a result, most employers have been in a position to manage their staffing problems rather than having to make do with the sporadic response of workers or applicants to the availability of work.

Back-to-work movements generally are no longer perceived as a viable source of labor for operation during a strike; in recent years, very few firms have even tried to encourage them.

The availability of an adequate internal supply of replacement labor is not an absolute necessity for successful exercise of the right to operate, however. Even though the hiring of replacements is typically seen as a risky venture, several firms have tried it with great success in virtually every case, much to the surprise of the company. The conclusion drawn by these firms from their own experience is that the hiring of replacements, like plant operation, is not as difficult a course of action as anticipated.

The growing ratio of white-collar to blue-collar employment in most industries suggests that a growing number of employers may find it possible to operate struck facilities by using internal sources of replacement labor. The apparent ease with which firms were able to hire outside replacements in recent years suggests an even more pervasive expansion in plant operation, although it remains to be seen whether the success in hiring replacements was a product of the loose labor market of the 1970s or the product of a more basic change in attitudes about working as a strikebreaker. In any event, the growing logistical feasibility of plant operation would seem to indicate that institutional problems and the fear of confrontation will come to play a relatively more prominent role as a restraint on the exercise of the right to operate in the years ahead.

Plant operation is a departure from the norm in union-management relations. As such, it represents a clear escalation of conflict and power by management in its relationship with a union. The response of a union to that action is likely to be a countervailing escalation of conflict and power, most notably in the form of violence in the short run and bitterness in the long run. These potential institutional problems constitute a formidable deterrent to operation.

The decision to undertake an escalation of power and conflict and accept the institutional costs of that action typically has been made on the basis of both pragmatic (economic) and philosophical (institutional) considerations. The decision to risk confrontation generally has had some pragmatic foundation in terms of avoiding potentially catastrophic losses of sales and customers. Rarely, however, has that decision been motivated by purely economic considerations; institutional considerations of the effect of operation on the union's short-run and long-run power and appeal also have significantly influenced the decision to operate. For the most part, however, plant operation has not been perceived or practiced as a weapon to enable an employer to break a union as well as to take a strike.

Employers that attempt to operate pay a price for such action in terms of short-run harassment, intimidation, and violence, and, to a lesser extent, long-run embarassment, bitterness, and retribution. That price, however, has not been as great as might have been expected given the extent to which plant operation threatens to alter the basic balance of power in a collective bargaining relationship.

One reason for this limited response of unions to plant operation has been the aversion of most employers to utilizing back-to-work movements or permanent replacements as a basis for manning a struck facility, thereby minimizing the threat of plant operation to the existence of striking unions and the livelihood of striking workers.

Thus far, the success and growing boldness of those firms in exercising their right to operate has not been challenged by a determined effort on the part of unions to raise the cost or lower the benefit of plant operation. The relatively limited tactical response of unions to the use of managerial and supervisory personnel as temporary replacements has been an important factor in making plant operation worthwhile in the short run and encouraging expanded use of that option in the long run. Any change in the mode of operation, however, may well alter that situation. Any significant expansion of plant operation, which still enjoys only limited popularity, may well provoke the opposition of the labor movement as a whole, which thus far has not been seriously threatened by the right of employers to operate.

The prospects for a basic change in the style or scale of plant operation are unclear. The surprising and growing ease of operation reported by most firms suggests that it is a more feasible option than has been realized. Nonetheless, plant operation and replacement hiring remain difficult and unpopular. It remains to be seen whether the pressure of growing foreign and domestic nonunion competition and the growing managerial resistance to unionization in most industries will significantly accelerate the trend toward plant operation. If it does, the response of unions and the labor movement to such a change also remains to be seen, but there can be little doubt that a response will be forthcoming. The possibilities in this respect are legion. They include government intervention in the form of legislation or regulation to restrict the right to operate or expand the right to boycott, and self-help measures such as sabotage, coalition bargaining, and organization of supervisory personnel.

APPENDIX

STRIKE/OPERATION
PLANNING GUIDELINES

I. STATEMENT OF POLICY

A. The company will take all reasonable measures to avoid strikes but will not hesitate to sustain one when, in the informed judgment of those responsible, the best interests of the business justify it. In the event of a strike, it is the policy of the company to operate its facilities to the extent feasible, taking into consideration the economics, the impact on labor relations and customers, and other factors.

B. The company recognizes the right of employees to engage in legal strikes but insists that its employees and their bargaining agents recognize the corresponding legal rights of the company as well as its property rights, including the rights of its agents, officials, and employees to have free entry and exit and to be free from violence or other illegal conduct directed against their persons or property. It is the policy of the company to take legal steps, as necessary, to ensure these rights, and to take disciplinary action against employees guilty of illegal conduct.

II. PRODUCTION PLANNING

A. It is the policy of the company that plants should plan to operate to the fullest extent possible during a strike or lockout. It is recognized, however, that this is not possible or economically practicable in all locations at all times. Therefore, a basic decision must be made first for each plant location as to the degree to which it will operate during a strike. This basic decision will include these alternatives or variations thereof.

1. Operate and ship at full capacity.

2. Operate and ship at reduced capacity.

3. Operate and ship only specific facilities/products.

4. Maintain facilities in standby condition.

5. Orderly shutdown.

B. There are numerous conditions that will influence the decision regarding plant operation. The basic factors to be considered in selecting a level of operation or which products are to be produced and in which order or quantity normally should include the following:

1. Protection of customers and market share.

2. Preservation of cash flow and profit contribution.

3. Feasibility of production given available manpower.

C. Based on the decision regarding plant operation, each location will prepare a strike plan. If it is not certain in advance which alternative will be followed, the location strike plan should provide for different possibilities. The following sections provide general guidance for the preparation of a location strike plan.

D. One factor that may have to be considered in deciding on level of operation and developing a strike plan is state unemployment compensation laws. In several states, strikers replaced during a strike are eligible for unemployment compensation. In at least one state, plants operating at or above 80 percent of capacity during a strike have been judged to have, in effect, replaced their striking workers, making them eligible for benefits.

E. Once a plan for operation is finalized, a plan for raw material procurement and storage should be developed, keeping in mind the possibility of restricted ingress and egress in the early stages of a strike. Special arrangements should be made with vendors regarding delivery schedules to assure "full" status for necessary materials, fuels, etc. and "empty" status for finished goods and waste materials at the time of contract expiration.

III. MANAGEMENT ORGANIZATION

A. Prior to and during a strike or lockout, it is essential that a management organization be established that will permit:

1. Proper decisions on production continuance.

2. Prompt decisions on bargaining.

3. Proper handling of work stoppage activities.

In most locations this organization may be identical to the one making daily decisions. In some locations, however, a new or different organization may have to be developed because of local organizational structures.

B. All functions and areas of responsibility should be clearly defined and put in writing. In addition, an appropriate organization chart should be developed for easy reference.

1. Assign an official historian. Have all facts reported to him. His job is to keep a chronological record of all pertinent events leading up to and occurring during the strike. He will also prepare a strike summary after the strike.

2. Assign responsibility for effective communication to customers, suppliers, striking employees, nonstriking employees, government agencies, and the public to specified individuals. One manager should be assigned sole spokesman for the plant in any public statements related to the strike, plant operation, or contract negotiations.

C. Determine which administrative and clerical functions will be essential under the operating plan and at what minimum level of staffing. Assess the likelihood that those functions can be carried out in-plant in the face of a strike and picket line and decide whether temporary headquarters are essential. If temporary headquarters are deemed essential, appropriate plans and arrangements are required several weeks in advance. Items to consider:

1. Number of offices and space of each

2. Telephones

3. Office equipment and supplies

4. Mail

5. Security

D. Preparation and distribution to appropriate management and staff personnel of lists of key personnel with their home and office addresses and telephone numbers is essential. This list, preferably in booklet form, should include key management and administrative personnel, local and international union representatives, company and union attorneys, offices of federal agencies such as the Federal Mediation and Conciliation Service (FMCS) and National Labor Relations Board (NLRB), numbers for federal, state, and local law enforcement agencies and the local fire department, as well as for any temporary offices that may be established.

IV. PRODUCTION MANNING

A. A tentative manpower schedule for planned level or levels of operation during a strike should be prepared well in advance of the contract expiration date. This requires a careful assessment of the number of positions. In determining the actual number of personnel needed, a two-shift schedule (twelve hours per day, seven days per week) can be considered at the outset to maximize the availability of locally trained personnel. A change to a three-shift schedule (twelve hours per day, ten days on, five days off, or some variation thereof) should be planned for as soon as sufficient experienced personnel from other locations can be brought in and/or local nonoperating personnel can be trained.

B. A careful and realistic skills inventory of all salaried (exempt and nonexempt) employees assigned to the plant should also be undertaken well in advance of contract expiration and continually updated as necessary. Based on this inventory, salaried personnel should be assigned to specific jobs for which they are qualified or can be trained. Those assignments should be communicated to salaried employees well in advance of contract expiration.

C. If, after all local salaried employees have been assigned to jobs, voids still exist in filling scheduled jobs, salaried employees will have to be obtained from other locations. Such personnel needs should be identified early to ensure the timely availability of the needed supplementary personnel. It is the responsibility of each location, with the assistance of divisional and, if necessary, corporate industrial relations staff, to recruit needed outside personnel.

D. When all positions have been filled by specific individuals from inside or outside the location, a careful assessment should be made of who may need training to ensure ability to perform adequately in the event of a strike. A plan for providing the necessary training should then be developed based on specific needs and local conditions. The possibility of hands-on training prior to contract expiration by having salaried employees observe and work with hourly employees on the job should be given serious consideration.

E. It may also be advisable to review and update training manuals for all jobs to be filled to reflect job changes and changes in technology and to make those manuals available to the appropriate salaried employee(s) prior to contract expiration.

F. In identifying training needs, careful attention must be paid to state operating license requirements. These requirements vary between states, but may include:

1. Boiler operator
2. Water treatment operator
3. Waste treatment operator
4. Weigh master
5. Truck driver
6. Welder
7. Electrician

The corporation maintains a companywide inventory of licensed salaried personnel in these areas, but primary responsibility for qualifying salaried personnel for necessary licenses remains with each location.

G. In addition to checking skills, professionals, trades, licenses, and, if appropriate, hobbies, considerable time and effort should be devoted to checking employees' physical conditions. Usually, twelve-hour shifts will be required. In addition, it may be necessary for employees manning the plant to live in the plant for an extended period. Thus, family circumstances may also have to be considered.

V. PERSONNEL SERVICES

A. While nonstriking employees cannot legally be prevented by union officials or other employees from entering or leaving the plant, the danger of this being done illegally always exists. Until free access to the plant can be assured, arrangements should be made to house and feed essential employees inside the plant and to provide protection to those who must come and go.

B. *Accommodations: On-site*

1. A thorough physical survey should be made of all existing offices, conference rooms, lounges, and other areas potentially suitable for sleeping quarters. Additional possibilities to be considered are:

   a. Pullman cars on plant sidings
   b. Ships or ferries for locations with dock facilities
   c. House trailers if permitted by zoning laws
   d. Campers if sanitary hookups are installed

2. A survey of existing shower and restroom facilities should also be made to determine adequacy for a live-in situation.

3. Living areas should be stocked with adequate quantities of cots, mattresses, blankets, sheets, and pillows. Arrangements should be made for laundry service with a firm that can be relied upon to cross a picket line, if necessary.

4. If possible, employees should be assigned sleeping locations on the basis of shift assignment to minimize disturbances. Each sleeping area should be numbered and a list of occupants posted. A master list of such assignments should be maintained by the personnel department for information and emergencies.

5. Arrangements for on-site sleeping accommodations should be checked with respect to local zoning laws and health regulations and should be inspected and approved by the local fire marshal.

C. *Accommodations: Off-site*

1. Arrangements will also have to be made to house employees from other locations off-site once access to the plant has been established.

2. To the extent feasible, it is advisable to concentrate the housing of outside employees for security reasons and to facilitate car pooling for travel to and from the plant.

3. Arrangements should be made with the motel to bill the plant directly for accommodations provided. Special arrangements may have to be made to schedule maid service at appropriate times (shift changes).

4. Consideration should be given to assignment of security guards to the facility where employees are housed and security should be one factor considered in the choice of the facility. In addition, it may be advisable in choosing a facility to consider the extent of general public access to the facility in order to limit the potential for incidents between salaried employees and strikers.

D. *Food Service: On-site*

1. Food service for salaried employees operating a struck facility should be of high quality and provided at company expense. General recommendations for food service are that all meals served be hot meals, a good variety of foods be served, and all meals be of high quality and adequate quantity.

2. The corporation maintains a list of vendors who specialize in providing food services to struck facilities that operate with salaried personnel. Other local vendors, however, may be utilized. In any event, it will be necessary to contact the vendor well in advance of contract expiration to determine:

   a. The number and schedule of meals to be provided.

   b. What additional or altered facilities will be needed for the vendor to prepare and serve meals.

   c. What arrangements must be made for the storage and shipment of food before and during a strike to ensure an adequate supply.

   d. Whether the vendor's employees will remain on-site and how they will be accommodated.

3. Careful attention should be given to determining what licenses and permits are required to prepare and serve meals on-site. If possible, food facilities should be inspected and approved by the local health department well in advance of the strike deadline.

E. *Entertainment and Recreation*

1. Serious consideration should be given to leisure time activity for employees housed in-plant, both for relaxation and physical fitness.

2. For relaxation, it is generally advisable to place television sets in various parts of the plant and to provide an adequate supply of lounge chairs for watching television, reading, or playing cards. Newspapers, magazines, paperback books, and playing cards should be available.

3. For recreation, provision of facilities and equipment for both outdoor (season permitting) sports such as volleyball, softball, horseshoes, and indoor activities such as Ping Pong, pool, darts, and air hockey may also prove to be a good investment.

4. For refreshment, it is important to have an adequate supply of soft drinks, gum, candy and cigarettes available at all times. In addition, consideration may be given to scheduling "happy hours" after each shift change. Before such action is taken, however, the legality of serving alcoholic beverages should be checked and a sound system for controlling the purchase, storage, and dispensing of those beverages should be devised.

F. *Other Services*

1. Employees assigned to work during the strike should be instructed to bring clothing and personal belongings into the plant prior to the strike deadline. Secure storage space should be made available, as necessary.

2. Employees assigned to work should be provided with work clothing and all necessary safety equipment. Adequate supplies should be purchased and securely stored in-plant before the strike deadline. Arrangements should be made for distribution, and employees informed of those arrangements.

3. It is also advisable to have a supply of soap, towels, razor blades, and other personal hygiene items in stock in the plant. In addition, some arrangement should be made for laundry service or facilities.

G. *Crossing the Picket Line*

1. A letter should be written to nonstriking employees in advance of the strike deadline outlining procedures to be followed in reporting to work and what to do if prevented from crossing the picket line. It is particularly important to advise nonstriking employees of the plant gates they may use and may not use either because they will be locked or because they are reserved for contractor personnel. In addition, it is important to advise employees as to how to cross a picket line. In general, the following rules are appropriate.

   a. Whenever possible, picket lines should be crossed in an automobile rather than on foot.

   b. Approach and cross picket line cautiously and at a slow rate of speed; do not be aggressive in any matter and avoid coming in contact with or inching against the body of a picket.

   c. Avoid extended conversations with pickets at the picket lines. Replies to questions or remarks should be courteous and brief.

   d. If detained by pickets, attempt to identify the persons involved and make careful note of the length of time detained, witnesses present, date, time, location, etc.

   e. Patience is the name of the game.

2. Law enforcement agencies should be requested to provide adequate police patrols and to be on call for assistance. Support

from local police may not be forthcoming or highly effective. Support from state police may be more effective but more difficult to secure since they may not be free to act until requested to do so by local authorities.

3. Plant guards should be stationed at all open gates to ensure safe access to the plant. The visible presence of observers and photographers at open gates also may facilitate employee access.

H. *Protection of Employees' Families*

1. Consideration may have to be given to providing car pool transportation for local nonstriking employees.

2. In smaller communities, patrols in the community by plant security personnel may serve to deter acts of vandalism and violence directed at nonstriking employees or their homes and families.

3. If harassing phone calls are made to the homes of nonstriking personnel, arrange with the telephone company for a locking device on the phone that enables calls to be traced. Even if not pursued, this can cut such calls drastically.

4. In extreme situations, it may be necessary to consider bodyguard protection for specific employees, their homes and/or families.

I. *Normally, strike preparations should not be concealed.*

VI. PERSONNEL POLICIES

A. All local salaried employees will be required to work, although there may be an occasional exception. If the spouse of a salaried employee is a member of the striking union and for personal reasons cannot work, the salaried employee may be granted a leave of absence without pay or benefits. If, in such a case, the salaried employee chooses to work, the assignment should be to a nonsensitive job.

B. All employees, whether local or from other locations, are under the direction of the manager of the struck location for the duration of their assignment to strike duty.

C. Whenever possible, out-of-town employees should be asked for a commitment to strike duty for the duration of the strike in order to reduce turnover and training costs. If this is not feasible, a commitment for no less than four weeks should be sought. In either event, to the extent possible, provision should be made to permit all working employees to return home every other weekend.

D. Each employee will receive his or her normal paycheck at his or her home location at the normal pay period. The employee should designate where the check is to be mailed. Additional pay for salaried employees will be distributed from the struck facility on the following basis.

1. *Eligibility for Overtime*

   a. Nonmanagerial employees are to be paid overtime and related premium payments as set forth below, regardless of whether the work performed is exempt or nonexempt in nature.

   b. Managerial employees are to be paid overtime and related premium payments only when the work performed is nonexempt in nature.

2. *Compensation*

   a. Any employee assigned to an hourly, daily, or monthly paid operating classification should be compensated at the hourly equivalent or the employee's normal rate for that classification, whichever is higher.

   b. Eligible employees are to be paid time and one-half the applicable salary for all hours worked in excess of eight consecutive hours, or eight hours in a calendar day, or forty hours per week, whichever is greatest.

   c. Eligible employees who are required to work on a scheduled day off will receive one and one-half times the applicable salary for all hours worked.

   d. Employees assigned to nonexempt positions who are eligible for overtime and premium payments and are required to live in a struck facility should receive compensation for certain time not normally regarded as working time. Pay for such employees who are *required by the company* to live in (as opposed to those who elect to live in but are free to leave when off duty) should be calculated on the basis of twenty-four hours worked per day, less the following offsets:
   Sleeping Period. An eight-hour period for sleeping should not be counted as time worked. If the sleeping period is interrupted by work demands, however, the interruptions must be counted as time worked. If the period is interrupted to such an extent that the employee cannot get at least five hours sleep during

the scheduled period, the entire period is working time.

Meal Periods. Besides sleeping periods, three hours "off duty" (meal periods, time spent for personal needs, and recreation) should not be counted as time worked. Only two and one-half hours should be offset for employees whose on-shift meal is eaten on "company time," however.

e. All employees regularly assigned to nonexempt work on shift schedules are to receive an applicable shift bonus for all appropriate hours. Such a bonus is to be computed at time and one-half for overtime hours.

f. Employees eligible for overtime and premium payments who are required to work on a holiday during a strike are to be paid for all such hours worked in accordance with local practice applicable to nonexempt employees.

g. Employees not eligible for overtime and premium payments who are required to work on a holiday are to be paid for that holiday at straight time based on their regular daily schedule during the strike.

h. Travel time (by the most direct route) to a struck location *outside the immediate area of the home* will be considered time worked and will be paid at the hourly equivalent of the employee's regular monthly salary. This time will be subject to Fair Labor Standards Act (FLSA) overtime provisions, if travel occurs in a workweek in which the employee is nonexempt.

E. All vacations at the struck location will be cancelled. If a vacation period is not able to be granted during the strike, employees should be given vacation time after the strike or, if they choose, may receive pay for the vacation time missed. In the event that it is not possible to grant vacation time missed because of a strike in the calendar year in which the strike occurs, that vacation time may be carried over to the following year.

F. Employee benefits will continue to be the same as coverage in the employee's home location. An employee's normal monthly salary for his or her permanent assignment should be used for benefit plan purposes except when an employee is assigned to a position with a higher rate.

G. The company will provide the necessary travel expenses to the struck facility and return for out-of-town employees. Airplane tickets and company or rental cars will be provided as necessary and appropriate. In addition, the following policies apply for personal expense reimbursement for loaned employees.

1. An employee who uses his personal automobile when assigned to a struck facility in the immediate area of his home location that is farther from his residence than his regular work location will be eligible for reimbursement for the difference in mileage, as incurred.

2. An employee may be authorized a round trip home at company expense. Such trips for an employee may not be authorized more often than every two weeks, except in the event of an emergency.

3. An employee's spouse may be authorized a trip to the struck location at company expense. Such trips must be in lieu of an authorized round trip for the employee to the home location and may not be authorized more often than once every four weeks. The amount of reimbursement for the spouse's transportation will be the cost of round trip airfare via coach class. Since this reimbursement will be considered taxable income to the employee, the amount will be increased by 25 percent for federal tax and required taxes will be withheld. Any other expenses incurred by the spouse in making the trip, including expenses while at the struck location, will be the responsibility of the employee.

4. Other personal expenses incurred by employees assigned from outside the immediate area will be reimbursed, as appropriate, under standard corporate policy. No expense reimbursement may be authorized for an employee during a period in which he would normally return to his or her home location but who elects to stay at the struck location.

H. The company will indemnify employees for all losses that are strike-related to the extent that such losses are not covered by insurance.

VII. EMPLOYEE RELATIONS

A. Once personnel policies and procedures have been set, they should be fully communicated and explained to all managers and to those employees, both local and loaned, who will be operating the facility. Those policies and procedures should be carefully adhered to and uniformly applied. Changes in or exceptions to established policy and procedure should be avoided unless absolutely necessary.

B. Before personnel are placed on the job, they should be thoroughly briefed on operating procedures and all safety rules. Particular attention should be given to familiarizing employees with any specific hazards to be encountered on their assigned job and with any protective equipment they may be required to wear.

C. Communication with employees is essential to the maintenance of morale. Thus, it is important to make full disclosure to salaried personnel of issues related to the strike and to keep them informed of progress in negotiations. In addition, it is important to keep them informed of what is going on in the plant. For that purpose, publication of a daily newsletter is recommended. Items that should be covered include:

1. Production levels—target and actual

2. Problems encountered, including breakdowns

3. Safety information and accident reports

D. It is generally advisable to identify one member of the personnel relations staff to serve as the contact point for employees with special problems, such as family emergencies, medical or legal problems, etc. That individual should also be available to answer questions regarding personnel policies and/or respond to complaints about those policies.

VIII. PLANT OPERATION

A. The decision as to whether to shut down and start up operations or take them over directly from hourly employees is a matter of local option. It is generally more efficient and effective, however, to take over operations directly. In any event, that will have to be the case for plant power facilities.

B. Precautions should be taken to reduce or eliminate the possibility of sabotage prior to shutdown or takeover of operations. Steps that may be taken include extra supervision or early shutdown or takeover by salaried personnel. In the event of shutdown or takeover, hourly employees released from their jobs may be kept in the plant or sent home but must be paid for their full scheduled shift in order to avoid any question of a lockout.

1. Any represented employee expressing an interest in continuing or returning to work should be advised that work is available, but under no circumstances should promises, threats, or other

inducements be made to encourage or discourage represented employees to continue or return to work.

C. Special steps may also have to be taken to provide for the safety of salaried employees on the job. In addition to initial and ongoing safety indoctrination, special personnel may have to be trained in treatment of minor injuries. Emergency first-aid kits should be located in designated areas, and steps taken to ensure the availability of a physician at all times. Special arrangements may also have to be made to ensure access to ambulance service in the event that it should be required.

D. In general, do not relax safety standards. Remember that the Occupational Safety and Health Act is still applicable. A union may try to get production stopped through this law by claiming undue hazard to the employees working and/or to the community because of an untrained or unqualified work force.

1. An adequate supply of all necessary personal protection equipment for working employees should be purchased and stored in-plant prior to the strike deadline.

E. All other federal, state, and local regulations also remain in effect. In particular, Environmental Protection Agency (EPA) emission and effluent standards must be met on a continuing basis. In addition, it may be necessary to secure state or local approval for on-site arrangements for temporary disposal of trash and solid waste.

F. It is also imperative to develop a fire protection plan for the facility as manned and operated in a strike. In general, this will require:

1. Training personnel to serve as a fire brigade.

2. Checking all equipment prior to a strike to ensure that it is in working order.

3. Checking sprinkler systems, fire alarms, and fire extinguishers prior to a strike.

4. It may also be advisable to alert local fire officials to the possibility of a strike and to seek a clear commitment on continued service.

G. Product quality standards should be maintained to the maximum extent possible. Changes in product quality should not be made without the specific approval of the customer, as well as the appropriate marketing and customer service functions. Extra attention may be necessary to ensure that quality standards are met.

H. Operation of a facility by salaried employees during a strike should be looked upon as a positive opportunity to review and evaluate hourly manning requirements.

IX. PLANT MAINTENANCE

A. Careful planning in the maintenance area is critical because of the importance of adequate maintenance in the successful operation of a struck facility.

1. Well in advance of contract expiration, all major maintenance requirements and schedules for the period following contract expiration should be reviewed. A determination should be made as to which of these requirements should be scheduled before the expiration date, which can be postponed or cancelled, and which will have to be performed during the strike.

2. Preventative maintenance schedules should also be reviewed to clearly identify work that must be done for safe continued operation.

3. Whenever possible, outside contract maintenance work should be completed prior to contract expiration.

B. The maintenance organization that will best serve a struck facility will vary with the complexity, size, and special needs of each location. It generally is advisable, however, to coordinate maintenance efforts through a central system and to staff the maintenance function for all operating shifts.

C. Generally, a maintenance force of about one-third of the normal hourly force should be sufficient to handle all but major, unforeseen problems. Part of this reduction is attributable to extended shifts. Additional reductions result because:

1. Operators can assist maintenance on major shutdowns and perform minor maintenance jobs while equipment is running.

2. Jurisdictional limits do not apply when salaried personnel perform maintenance.

3. Engineering ingenuity comes into play.

D. A determination of the numbers and skills of maintenance workers required and a survey of what skills are available at the plant location should be completed well in advance of the contract expiration date.

The early identification of skill shortages is essential to permit time to locate qualified, available loaned personnel. When such personnel are in short supply, it may be necessary to consider on-the-job training using a "helper approach."

E. Prepare a complete list of tools required by the maintenance work force and plan to have these tools and a sufficient supply of tool boxes available at the time of contract expiration. Plans should also be made for distribution and control of tools.

F. The use of contract maintenance, when possible, can help overall maintenance coverage and reduce manpower needs. Off-site facilities should be surveyed and arrangements made to cover as many needs as possible, such as automotive, electric motor, and pump repairs. The use of contract maintenance in-plant is also a possibility, but one that depends on the ability of the contractor to ensure that his employees will cross a picket line. Contractors and/or suppliers performing bargaining-unit work during a strike are not protected by statutory prohibitions of secondary boycott activity.

X. PLANT SECURITY

A. A complete security survey should be made of the facility before contract expiration in order to identify potential problem areas or points of vulnerability. The survey should include a review of all entrances and boundaries at the location as well as off-site facilities. Repairs should be made or precautions taken where areas of vulnerability are detected. Some of the things to be considered are:

1. Check all fences and gates and make repairs where necessary.

2. Review and survey all boundary lines and remote sites and identify vulnerable areas such as unfenced sections, pipelines, substations, storage areas, outside warehouses, etc. Determine how these areas can best be protected in the event of a strike.

3. Utility connections are particularly important potential points of vulnerability. Power supply feeders and purchased power transformers are very vulnerable to sabotage and extra precautions may have to be taken to protect these facilities. Similarly, water-pumping stations, mains, and purification facilities which are remotely located may present special security problems, as will exposed pipeline connections of any type.

4. Check lighting of plant perimeter and provide additional lighting where required. Mesh shielding may be required to protect lights from slingshots, rocks, air guns, etc.

5. Identify likely picket areas and clear obstructions to these areas to allow effective surveillance, as appropriate. Make sure that property lines in these areas are clearly marked.

6. Identify all avenues of entry to the location and determine which, if any, should be closed in the event of a strike, which should be used by company employees, and which are most suitable for use by contractor employees.

B. On the basis of the results of the security survey, a determination should be made of the number and disposition of security personnel required to maintain a secure facility. Regular security guards may need to be supplemented by hiring or contracting for additional security personnel. Whenever such personnel are retained, it is vital to ensure that they are adequately trained and licensed. In general, it is recommended that all security personnel be uniformed, but they should not carry firearms except in extraordinary circumstances. The use of guard dogs is a possibility worthy of consideration, particularly at remote sites or at isolated sections of the location.

C. An effective communications system should be set up for security personnel in order to maintain contact with guards around the facility at all times. It is also important to ensure communication with local law enforcement authorities in the event of problems with telephone service.

D. Prior to contract expiration, contact should be made with local and state law enforcement agencies to inform them of the potential strike situation and of the possibility of unlawful activity. Commitments for assistance in the form of regular patrols and/or a rapid-response capability should be sought. One individual should be designated to be the primary contact between the facility and police officials.

E. Guard posts and patrol routes should be determined in advance of contract expiration. Fixed positions should be placed to allow visibility of wide areas and to protect entrances or other vulnerable areas such as substations or pump houses. Roving patrols should cover areas where constant security is impractical, such as the perimeter of the facility and remote sites. Irregular routes and times are advisable to avoid predictability.

F. An effective system for surveillance and documentation of strike-related activity can be helpful in deterring illegal activity and is essential in obtaining restraining orders against such activity.

1. Two-man teams equipped with notebooks, tape recorders, and polaroid cameras should be assigned to specific observation points.

2. Consideration should be given to using a TV camera to tape illegal picket activity. TV cameras equipped with a time-date generator that automatically reads date and time on the film as it is shot are particularly effective.

3. Thirty-five millimeter camera equipment, including telescopic lenses, high-power flash attachments, and high-speed film can be useful in photographing illegal activity but lack the action effect of TV.

4. In areas where such equipment may be necessary, high-power telescopes and/or night vision binoculars should be considered.

G. Where practical, some arrangements should be made for clearing roadways around entrances of nails and other debris. A street sweeper may be necessary, as magnets will not pick up aluminum nails.

H. Consideration should also be given to establishing a capability to monitor and record CB radio transmissions.

XI. TRANSPORTATION

A. In the event of a strike and a decision to operate the facility, it is essential that careful attention be given to arrangements to ensure continuity of supply and shipment. Significant problems in this area must be anticipated and plans made to deal with those problems.

B. *Rail Transportation*

1. Arrange and confirm that railroad supervision will perform necessary switching work. Expose company salaried personnel to switching needs, locations, and techniques sufficiently to enable them to supplement railroad personnel should that be necessary.

2. Prepare a minimum switch service schedule. Establish twenty-four-hour controls to coordinate and service.

3. Have all switch engines and trackmobiles in top operating condition. Train salaried personnel as needed to operate this equipment.

4. Provide security checks of tracks, and switches in particular.

5. Establish and maintain liaison with railroad security personnel.

C. *Truck Transporation*

1. Develop a list of operators who will guarantee service even if it means crossing a picket line.

2. Negotiate and confirm service arrangements including off-site exchange. Several transfer points may need to be set up where drivers and/or tractors can be switched. It may be necessary to provide security guards for these locations.

3. Identify equipment and personnel needs:

   a. Acquire tractors and equipment (hoses, tires, fittings).

   b. Select, train, and license necessary company personnel.

   c. Provide for personnel needed to secure truck shipments (in-truck observers, truck trailers, and security cars).

4. Keep trucking companies informed of problems and picket activities. Advise as to best means of approach and entrance on a daily basis.

D. *Other Means of Transportation*

1. Problems may also be encountered in shipment of inbound and outbound materials by water. If possible, nonunion operators and personnel should be identified. Boat picketing should be anticipated.

2. Explore possibility of delivery by helicopter of key material and personnel.

E. *Material Handling*

1. Provide alternative truck and rail unloading and loading sites and capability in case one of the other shipment methods is closed.

2. Select and train unloading personnel; where such work involves heavy physical exertion it may be advisable to provide for extra manpower.

XII. CUSTOMERS AND SUPPLIERS

A. In a strike situation management must, of course, consider the effects on customers and suppliers. From a labor relations viewpoint, it is company policy to operate plants. Such action should also enable the company to gain substantial credit from its customers and suppliers for minimizing the breaks or voids in the flow of materials.

B. It is important that sales personnel maintain close personal liaison with customers, both immediately preceding and during a strike, to offer assurances of continued production and shipment of goods. Specific matters to be discussed include:

1. Progress of negotiation and status of operations.

2. Quality assurances—possible changes in products.

3. Possible order restrictions or changes in delivery schedules.

4. Possible changes in method of shipment.

5. Possible adjustment of customer inventory prior to contract expiration.

C. Notification should be sent to vendors that a strike is imminent when that appears to be the case. This notification typically should address the following areas:

1. Delay of or no delay of shipments if a strike begins.

2. Possible necessity to establish different lead times or delivery schedules for orders.

3. Possible necessity to ship to a different location or by a different mode of transportation.

D. Outside contractors performing work in the plant should be expected to continue to work despite the existence of a strike and so informed prior to contract expiration. A separate reserved gate for use by contractor personnel should be established and clearly marked prior to contract expiration. Only employees of contractors not doing bargaining-unit work should be permitted to use the reserved gate, and security personnel should be assigned to ensure that this rule is strictly enforced.

XIII. COMMUNICATIONS

A. Timely, factual, and effective communications is a significant factor in successful plant operation. This requires a plan, organization, equipment, and supplies and clear identification of individual responsibilities.

B. Prior to contract expiration, steps should be taken to ensure adequate communications capability in the event of a strike. Specifically, alternative arrangements may have to be made for delivery of mail, and salaried employees trained to operate telephone switchboards. Duplicating equipment and supplies and public address systems should also be checked.

C. Effective internal communication is essential to maintain morale and operating efficiency. Such communication should begin well in advance of a possible strike and continue throughout the course of operation. Specific steps might include:

1. Establish expanded daily production meetings to include all basic management functions.

2. Establish a daily newsletter and identify special bulletin boards for posting updates.

3. Establish an internal hotline for salaried employees and their families to call and receive a recorded information update.

4. Communicate with families of people working. This has a good effect on morale, especially when those people are living in the plant.

5. Maintain visibility and accessibility of top management to working employees. This also can have a good effect on morale.

D. In general, it is company policy to maintain a low public profile during a strike and operation. There are many types of unusual circumstances that may occur and to overreact to one or many of them may jeopardize the morale of employees and/or the impact of plant operation. It is, however, recognized that the fact of a strike and operation cannot be ignored by the media and local government and community leaders.

1. One individual should be designated as the sole spokesman for the facility in making any public statements about the strike or plant operation.

2. News releases may be necessary or advisable on a regular or ad hoc basis. In making such releases, the following should be considered:

   a. Avoid acting as a spokesman for the union.

   b. Deal in facts—keep in mind the importance of long-range employee relations.

    c. Remind the public that the physical act of stopping production was taken by the union.

    d. All releases must be cleared by the company negotiators.

3. Consideration should be given to establishing an external hotline for hourly employees and the public to call to receive a recorded information update.

XIV. RECORDS AND EVIDENCE

A. A complete, accurate history of a work stoppage should be maintained. This includes basic information such as lost man-hours and detailed accounts of illegal picket activity.

B. A strike information and control committee should be established. The objective of the committee is to ensure that adequate records and evidence relating to the strike are obtained. This committee should continue as long as there is any evidence of misconduct or illegal activity by pickets.

C. The committee should direct and be responsible for the work of those assigned to observe and record picket line activity. It should receive and review all reports of picketing incidents from observers, employees, and others and prepare a daily report on picket activity and other related developments.

D. A local attorney, competent in labor law, should be retained in advance of any work stoppage, but only after consultation with corporate counsel.

E. A complete strike history should be maintained. This history should include meetings held, telephone calls or visits by union representatives or government officials, emergencies or acts of vandalism, etc.

F. A complete accounting of all strike-related expenses should be maintained. These expenses would include attorney fees, communication problems, equipment rentals, security services, property damage, etc.

XV. LEGAL CONSIDERATIONS

A. *Legal Counsel*

    1. To ensure that company representatives conduct themselves in a legal and ethical manner during a strike, and that all other

parties conduct themselves within applicable federal and state laws, legal guidance should be obtained from three sources:

   a. Division counsel

   b. Corporate labor counsel

   c. A competent local attorney specializing in labor-management relations

2. It will be the responsibility of division counsel to:

   a. Act as legal advisor to the local management organization in non-labor matters;

   b. Recommend to the local management organization a suitable local attorney and arrange for his services;

   c. Ensure adequate property insurance coverages and handle claims for vandalism damage.

3. It will be the responsibility of corporate labor counsel to:

   a. Act as a counsultant to the local management organization in labor matters;

   b. Check strike preparation plans and activities for possible law violations;

   c. Contact the NLRB regional office to establish lines of communication and request that all matters such as unfair labor practice charges be referred to him.

4. It will be the responsibility of the outside attorney to:

   a. Establish preliminary contact with the clerk of the circuit court and the sheriff to arrange for quick issuance and service of process in large volume on short notice, if possible;

   b. Be prepared with legal research and preliminary drafting of complaints, briefs, and legal process to seek injunctive relief in event mass picketing or violence occurs;

   c. Make certain that all evidence relating to picketing or any misconduct is being assembled in usable form;

   d. Represent the company in all legal proceedings except before the NLRB.

B. *Rules of Conduct for Management*

1. Company representatives are always privileged to communicate with striking employees for the purpose of expressing their

opinions and reporting facts, as long as they make no promises or threats; however, the solicitation of individual strikers to abandon a strike and return to work may also constitute unlawful conduct.

2. As a practical matter, company representatives need not be unduly concerned over the possibility that some conduct on their part may be alleged to be an unfair labor practice. Nevertheless, it is the company's policy in a labor dispute to take only actions that are legally permissible.

3. It is permissible to:

   a. Explain to employees the benefits they presently enjoy, the terms of the latest offer, and how well they will compare with employees of other companies;

   b. Urge another vote on the offer;

   c. Caution employees about the disadvantages of a strike—the loss of income, the requirement to serve on a picket line, and the right of the company to hire replacements;

   d. Correct any untrue or misleading statements made by the union;

   e. Advise employees of their legal right to refrain from striking;

   f. Enforce normal plant rules with strikers just as with nonstriking employees;

   g. Put into effect for any bargaining-unit employees who may be working during the strike the terms of the company's most recent offer to the union;

   h. State that the plant is open and that work is available during the strike.

4. It is unlawful to:

   a. Refuse to bargain after the strike begins;

   b. Insist that the strike be abandoned as a condition for resuming bargaining;

   c. Promise strikers (or grant to bargaining-unit employees who may be working) a wage increase or improvement in benefits or terms not previously offered to the union in negotiations;

    d. Bargain individually with employees, even on minor matters;

    e. Tell strikers that they will be "discharged," "terminated," "considered to have resigned," or "regarded as new employees" if they fail to return to work;

    f. Threaten to close or move the plant or to reduce drastically operations;

    g. Spy on union meetings;

    h. Threaten any sort of reprisal for striking;

    i. Take pictures of peaceful picketing for the purpose of intimidating pickets;

    j. Call individuals or small groups of employees into supervisors' offices for antiunion speeches;

    k. Make false statements about the union;

    l. Discourage membership in or support of the union;

    m. Ask how a striker voted.

C. *Replacement of Economic Strikers*

1. In an economic strike, there is no legal bar to the employer's hiring permanent replacements for the strikers. Once he has been permently replaced, a striker is entitled to reinstatement only as future job openings occur.

2. The wisdom of a replacement program is dependent upon a number of factors, including:

    a. The number and skills of the employees needed;

    b. The availability of workers and skills in the community;

    c. Wage levels;

    d. Labor climate in the area;

    e. The possibility of boycotting of products by customers or customers' employees.

3. If the decision is made to replace strikers, the following principles should be observed:

    a. Because a striking employee has a legal right individually to abandon the strike and return to work and because, from a standpoint of skills and training investment, he ordinarily is a much more desirable employee than a new one, it is usually advisable (although not required) to invite striking employees to return before hiring replacements.

b. The communication to striking employees should:

    (1) Be carefully phrased to avoid coercion or any appearance of discouraging membership in or support of the union;

    (2) Be in the form of a certified letter to the home of each employee;

    (3) Explain the mutual rights of the parties;

    (4) Stress the economic reasons for hiring to resume or increase production;

    (5) Avoid use of the words "terminated" or "discharged" and use only "replaced";

    (6) Set a deadline for the start of hiring permanent replacements. State that failure to report on or before that date will be taken as an indication that the employee does not wish to return to work and that the company is free to hire a replacement.

c. Hire replacements from among available applicants, advertise in appropriate newspapers for replacements for strikers, or use regular private employment agencies. The U.S. and most state employment services will not refer workers to fill strikers' jobs.

d. If applicants are interviewed away from the plant, they should be advised of the strike and picketing.

e. Tell the replacements that they are being hired on a permanent basis and, if they prove to be satisfactory employees, will not be displaced by returning strikers after the work stoppage.

f. Use the same wage rate brackets for the replacement employees; do not pay higher rates.

g. Within each job classification, prepare a list of employees in seniority order, replace the employees in inverse order of seniority until all employees in the classification have been replaced, have the records show that a particular employee, by name, was replaced by a particular new employee, by name.

h. Send a letter to the last known address of the replaced striker stating, "You have been permanently replaced." Date and mail the letter the day the replacement is hired.

D. *Unemployment Compensation for Strikers*

1. In most states, a striking employee (including employees who voluntarily recognize a picket line established by a striking union) is not eligible for unemployment compensation benefits. (A few states pay striking employees after a waiting period.) Strikers who have been permanently replaced and workers who have been locked out, however, may be eligible for benefits under state law. In at least one state, striking workers at a plant operating in excess of 80 percent of normal capacity have been ruled to have been effectively replaced and, therefore, eligible for benefits.

2. To minimize the possibility that strikers will be ruled eligible, the following steps are to be taken:

   a. Within three days after the start of the strike, notify the appropriate unemployment compensation office of the strike, enclosing a list of the names and social security numbers of all strikers.

   b. All employees (strikers and nonstrikers) are to be advised that the plant is open and that they are expected to report for work as usual.

   c. Supervisors are to be instructed that they are not even to suggest that work is not available during the strike.

   d. Regular employee gates are to be kept open.

   e. Employees reporting for work are to be admitted.

   f. Timecards are to be placed in the regular racks.

   g. Normal starting whistles are to be blown.

   h. If the plant is not operating, power necessary to operate machinery should be ready to turn on.

   i. Supervisors are to be stationed in their regular places, ready to put anyone to work who reports.

   j. Any claims by striking employees for benefits are to be challenged.

k. Employees on layoff status prior to the strike are to be advised by letter that the plant is open and that they are recalled for work. If they do not report within one week, their continuing claims for benefits should be challenged.

E. *Lockouts*

1. A lockout is the closing of a plant or other denial of employment by an employer for the purpose of exerting economic pressure on the employees or the union in support of the employer's bargaining position. The Supreme Court has ruled that an "offensive" lockout by an employer, after reaching an impasse in bargaining, is not unlawful. Further, the NLRB has ruled that it is not necessary to reach a bargaining impasse before an employer can legally lock out, provided the lockout is not "inherently prejudicial to union interests" and provided that the employer had "significant economic justification."

2. In any contract negotiation, the possible use of the lockout should be thoroughly considered, the same as any other legal weapon available. Advice of labor counsel is essential in advance, however. The possibility of operation using company personnel during a lockout should also be considered.

Index of Cases

Index

Racial Policies of American Industry Series

Order from: Kraus Reprint Co., Route 100, Millwood, New York 10546

STUDIES OF NEGRO EMPLOYMENT

Vol. I.   *Negro Employment in Basic Industry: A Study of Racial Policies in Six Industries (Automobile, Aerospace, Steel, Rubber Tires, Petroleum, and Chemicals),* by Herbert R. Northrup, Richard L. Rowan, et al.   1970.   *

Vol. II.   *Negro Employment in Finance: A Study of Racial Policies in Banking and Insurance,* by Armand J. Thieblot, Jr., and Linda Pickthorne Fletcher.   1970.   *

Vol. III.   *Negro Employment in Public Utilities: A Study of Racial Policies in the Electric Power, Gas, and Telephone Industries,* by Bernard E. Anderson.   1970.   *

Vol. IV.   *Negro Employment in Southern Industry: A Study of Racial Policies in the Paper, Lumber, Tobacco, Coal Mining, and Textile Industries,* by Herbert R. Northrup, Richard L. Rowan, et al.
1971. $13.50

Vol. V.   *Negro Employment in Land and Air Transport: A Study of Racial Policies in the Railroad, Airline, Trucking, and Urban Transit Industries,* by Herbert R. Northrup, Howard W. Risher, Jr., Richard D. Leone, and Philip W. Jeffress.   1971. $13.50

Vol. VI.   *Negro Employment in Retail Trade: A Study of Racial Policies in the Department Store, Drugstore, and Supermarket Industries,* by Gordon F. Bloom, F. Marion Fletcher, and Charles R. Perry.
1972. $12.00

Vol. VII.   *Negro Employment in the Maritime Industries: A Study of Racial Policies in the Shipbuilding, Longshore, and Offshore Maritime Industries,* by Lester Rubin, William S. Swift, and Herbert R. Northrup.   1974.   *

Vol. VIII.   *Black and Other Minority Participation in the All-Volunteer Navy and Marine Corps,* by Herbert R. Northrup, Steven M. DiAntonio, John A. Brinker, and Dale F. Daniel.   1979. $18.50

Order from the Industrial Research Unit
The Wharton School, University of Pennsylvania
Philadelphia, Pennsylvania 19104

* Order these books from University Microfilms, Inc., Attn: Books Editorial Department, 300 North Zeeb Road, Ann Arbor, Michigan 48106.